COPING
WITH LIFE
AFTER YOUR
MATE DIES

COPING
WITH LIFE
AFTER YOUR
MATE DIES

Second Edition

**Donald C. Cushenbery
and Rita Crossley Cushenbery**

Baker Books

A Division of Baker Book House Co
Grand Rapids, Michigan 49516

© 1991, 1997 by Donald C. Cushenbery and Rita Crossley Cushenbery

Published by Baker Books
a division of Baker Book House Company
P.O. Box 6287, Grand Rapids, MI 49516-6287

Fourth printing, March 2002

Printed in the United States of America

Library of Congress Cataloging-in-Publication Data

Cushenbery, Donald C.
  Coping with life after your mate dies / Donald C. Cushenbery and Rita Crossley Cushenbery. — 2nd ed.
    p.   cm.
  Includes bibliographical references.
  ISBN 0-8010-5765-5 (pbk.)
    1. Grief—Religious aspects—Christianity. 2. Widowers—Conduct of life. 3. Widows—Conduct of life. I. Cushenbery, Rita Crossley. II. Title.
BV4905.2.C87   1997
248.8'66—dc21   97-8996

Scripture quotations are from the Revised Standard Version of the Bible, copyright 1946, 1952, 1971 by the Division of Christian Education of the National Council of the Churches of Christ in the USA. Used by permission.

For current information about all releases from Baker Book House, visit our web site:
                    http://www.bakerbooks.com

Contents

1050

114092

Preface

This volume represents a new and revised edition of our original book, *Coping with Life after Your Mate Dies* (Baker Book House, 1991). Our updated version presents additional information in an exciting new format to help persons with the process of dealing with the intense hurt of the death of a spouse. Some of the principles highlighted in the various chapters may also be applied to the hurt surrounding the death of other close family members or the event of separation or divorce.

Our new book is not intended solely as a general devotional guide as is the case with many books dealing with grief. You are a busy person, and with that in mind we have worked deliberately to place all of our pertinent information in a clear, practical, brief, and easy-to-read format. Hundreds of people who bought and read our original volume liked it for these features. We focus our attention on a topic and attempt to give you step-by-step suggestions for dealing with certain issues. We have tried to be frank, caring, and helpful with our advice. It is our sincere desire that our book will assist you with dealing with your grief.

Death is a topic that most of us would rather not discuss. In the case of married couples, one of the partners will most likely die before the other. We have a tendency not to discuss death, and we somehow want to believe that death occurs in families other than our own.

Whether or not you are a Christian, the event of physical death is inevitable and final. The surviving spouse recognizes that his or her life will change in many ways. There will be no more happy times together when vacations are taken or when children and grandchildren are visited. Gone are the times when the joys and challenges of daily life are shared with a loving mate.

There are many things about death that we do not understand, and most people have a dreadful fear of the unknown. Though Christians have a spiritual understanding that the deceased mate is now in heaven, they cannot entirely know or comprehend the exact details about the afterlife. All of us recognize that with each passing day we are nearer to our own death and eternal destiny. For example, if you have already selected a cemetery plot, you are painfully aware of the eventual day when the ground will be opened for the entrance of your body or that of your spouse. Even so, you may have many perplexing questions.

The death of a mate is especially painful for couples who have lived closely for many years or who have young children. The survivor may feel that God no longer cares, or else he would have intervened and stopped the impending death of the loved one.

No one escapes physical death. It cannot be overcome with money, influence, community status, or political power. The billionaire is affected in the same manner as a homeless person. Most survivors are not ready to face the entire reality of everyday living following the death of their mate, as Rita and I discovered following the deaths of our spouses.

It is our desire that after you read this book, you will have a better understanding of how to cope with the death of your mate. We hope our comments will help you to be a survivor and to live a triumphant life with the continuing understanding that God is the same—yesterday, today, and forever.

Acknowledgments

*M*any persons helped us critique the original volume and the present revised edition. Over two dozen friends of varying ages who have lost their spouses gave us helpful suggestions for improving our material. These data were compiled from face-to-face interviews, telephone conversations, and remarks in writing. The book is better because they had a common belief that a volume of this nature was greatly needed.

Dee Fogarty prepared the final manuscript on the word processor. She has our gratitude for supplying us with a very acceptable product. My dear granddaughter, Becky Tatreau, gave ideas to me regarding various topics dealing with the Internet and America Online.

We also wish to thank hundreds of unnamed persons who have been in our many workshops and lecture audiences for encouraging us along the way. Nearly every individual knew of some friend or loved one who needed the book *now*. Finally, we acknowledge the legacy left by Elfrieda Cushenbery and Dick Crossley, our departed spouses, whose presence enriched so many years of our lives.

Introduction

*R*ita's husband, Dick, died in October 1985. My wife, Elfrieda, died in September 1988. At those times, even though we were believers, we were immediately left with a deep sense of loss.

We looked in bookstores for a good book relating to grief, but we found that most books were general and devotional in nature and did not help us with the specific day-to-day challenges of a survivor. When both of us retired as teachers in 1989, we were impressed with the suggestion of many of our caring friends that we write a book just for those who had lost a mate. Some felt that since I had been a university professor and author of many publications as well as an interim pastor, I should have the skills for the project. Rita has counseled hurting persons for many years. However, we felt our most important qualification was that we had experienced firsthand the death of a mate.

Coping with Life after Your Mate Dies was first published in 1991 and enjoyed a wide circulation thereafter. By 1996, it became quite clear that an updated, revised edition with additional and more current suggestions for grieving mates was needed. We hope this new edition will receive the same wide support as our original book enjoyed.

The chapters and material for this volume have been constructed with the idea that they can be read in a short period of time with a high level of interest. This book is intended for survivors of all ages, not just seniors. Some topics and material from the original edition have been changed, and new subjects and recommendations have been included in the revised edition to make it conform to our high standards of publication.

Some of the chapters have actual case studies to illustrate certain principles. The new edition contains updated and expanded examples to make the text even more meaningful and helpful. To protect the privacy of the persons involved, all names and some minor details have been changed or disguised.

Living with the Grief

*A*ccording to an old saying, two facts of life are inevitable: death and taxes. Regardless of one's present financial and social status, these two events will most surely come to pass. The man or woman who is worth several billion dollars faces his or her last breath just as surely as the homeless person who may be living under a bridge or in a shack beside a dirt road.

Many people set aside the thought of death because the only time they are confronted with it is at a funeral for an elderly friend or relative who lived a long, satisfying life. But we all know that life is fragile and that the sudden crash of an airplane or car or a devastating illness can result in the shattered hopes and dreams of people of any age. Many of our readers will remember the ValuJet plane crash in the Florida Everglades near Miami in May 1996. The 110 people aboard who were bound for Atlanta had no idea that their lives would be lost when the plane nose-dived into the swamp. Most of the bodies were not intact and could not be identified. These persons did not have a second chance. Dozens of relatives were thrown into unexpected grief. Entire families were killed. The grief will last a lifetime for the surviving spouses.

We have no assurance of how long we might live, despite medical technology and all our efforts to prolong life with proper exercise and good, prudent living habits. I knew a man who was an avid, dedicated marathon runner and who ate only "natural" foods that he purchased at a specialty food store. His blood pressure was usually around 110 over 70—a reading more typical of a teenager than of a forty-nine-year-old man. Yet, while making his usual three-mile run one morning, he was killed suddenly by a drunken driver who had failed to stop at a red light. The physically fit runner left a sorrowing widow with three school-age children.

During your lifetime, you have no doubt experienced the loss of one or more loved ones, but the loss of a mate is overwhelmingly traumatic. You are probably reading this book because you have recently been confronted with the death of your mate and with the stark realities of loneliness, lack of companionship, and the practical concerns that follow such an event.

Whether or not your mate was a Christian, the present hurt of his or her absence is still very evident. For some people, the intense grieving process may last six months to two years; for others, dealing with the loss may continue until their own deaths. The length of time each individual needs for grief resolution depends on several factors. If the death was sudden or totally unexpected, the period of grief may extend for a considerable length of time. Then, too, the degree of dependence you placed on your mate is significant. For example, a husband may have assumed complete charge of the financial aspects of the marriage, including the writing of all checks. If he dies suddenly, his wife may be plunged into intense, prolonged depression because she does not have the confidence or training for making important financial decisions. On the other hand, the degree and length of the period of mourning may be lessened if the survivor has workable coping skills and is surrounded by many caring friends and neighbors.

Dealing with a severe crisis such as the death of a mate is softened to the degree that you bring your feelings and expectations in line with Jesus' teachings. That means waiting and trusting in God and his long-range plan for your life. Learn a lesson from Job, who sat on an ash heap for a long period of time. To be spiritually alive and mentally productive, we all need to undergo some pruning and refining before we can experience victorious Christian living. Trying to analyze every negative element in your life has no purpose if you trust fully in God. Scripture tells us, "Trust in the LORD with all your heart, and do not rely on your own insight" (Prov. 3:5). The first step is to immerse yourself in the Word and believe it.

There are several basic principles that you should remember as you deal with your grief. Recognizing and understanding these aspects will help you place the whole mourning process in its proper perspective. We emphasize these items at this point because there appears to be considerable misunderstanding concerning them—as evidenced by some of the remarks made by the widows and widowers Rita and I have met.

1. *It is both proper and sensible to grieve.* It may bother some people to see you cry, but that is their problem, not yours! God gives us tears and understands that they are a necessary part of healing. They do not imply that you do not trust in God. Even Jesus wept over the death of his friend Lazarus. Grief is one of the most common emotions of any human being, whether believer or nonbeliever. It is certainly normal to express sorrow for the loss of a mate, and it would be unnatural to treat that

death as merely a passing event, a temporary inconvenience to be handled without feeling. The wife of an acquaintance of ours died nearly six years ago. The widower has not moved a single item among her belongings and in many ways gives the impression that he is hoarding a large deposit of unresolved grief. Many professional therapists contend that lingering grief that is not dealt with may lead to long-term depression and other serious physical and emotional problems.

Unfortunately, some people have the idea that they should not show outward signs of grieving because some of their friends might think that they lacked faith or courage to live a triumphant life. Furthermore, some persons may "assign" a length of time for grieving. Let me illustrate. My friend Michelle lost her husband in a light plane crash at the age of forty-seven. Two years later she confided to me that some of her friends had told her that she should not be "weepy" anymore because she needed to be "strong" and get on with her life. She seemed greatly relieved when I told her that I felt it was quite appropriate for her to display any reaction she liked, such as crying on her late husband's birthday.

In summary, dealing with grief is an individual matter, and the griever is finally responsible for his or her level of loss. If it is therapeutic to mention your late husband's or wife's name during a conversation, don't be hesitant to do so.

2. *It is not a sign of personal weakness to seek help from others during your bereavement.* The death of a loved one constitutes a major event in the life of any caring human being. Unless you are exceptional and are endowed with precise coping skills, there is a good chance that you will need help in adjusting to a new life. Nearly every large hospital has a chaplain's office. Many times hospital clergypersons conduct workshops for people in bereavement. Check with local hospital administrators about

these opportunities. Many agencies are anxious to help you. These groups are valuable regardless of your present age. They are not just for older widows or widowers.

One of the national groups available is T.H.E.O.S. (They Help Each Other Spiritually). Their international headquarters are at 1301 Clark Building, 717 Liberty Avenue, Pittsburgh, Pennsylvania 15222 (Phone: 412 471-7799; Fax: 412 471-7782). Contact them to find the closest T.H.E.O.S. group to your home. They also publish a magazine and other materials that are very helpful. Check with your local Visiting Nurse Association to see if they conduct bereavement workshops. Check your Yellow Pages for information.

If you are connected to America Online, there are several possibilities for joining with individuals and groups concerned with coping with the death of a spouse. Examine the latest edition of World Wide Web Yellow Pages for the web sites of various groups concerned with grief. It is also possible to engage in forum chat groups with other persons like yourself. You might consider leaving a message on the announcement board stating the desire to communicate with others who are grieving. E-mail messages will often come back to you in a short time. In fact, some persons have actually used e-mail for a long-term social relationship with another individual in a distant part of the country. A grieving widow or widower in another area may provide some useful suggestions for dealing with your particular situation. The cost of America Online and similar services is quite modest in most cases.

Most large city newspapers carry announcements of the place and time of meetings of various support groups. Call the social editor of the paper for information. For example, the following groups meet regularly in Omaha: Compassionate Friends, Survivors of Suicide, and Widowed Mutual Help Group. If you live in a small town or rural area, check with your county social services department for recommendations about support groups. If necessary, you can contact county and regional mental health centers for recommendations about individual and group counseling opportunities. On a more personal level, be open to the support offered by family members and friends.

3. *The crisis of grief may serve as a stimulus for you to get involved in creative activities, both in and out of the church.* The longer you isolate yourself from friends and neighbors, the longer the grieving period may last. The volunteer who works as a nurse's aide in a hospital soon learns that there are many people who are encountering both physical and emotional hurts. Such experiences can show that death seems a blessing when it finally occurs at the end of a prolonged illness. Families who for years have stood by the bedside of a comatose loved one may attest that there are things worse than death.

4. *Your grief is different in significant ways from that experienced by others.* A longtime Christian friend who had lost his wife came to me shortly after Elfrieda's funeral and said, "I know just how you are feeling. I buried my wife last year." I didn't say so, but I had the notion to mention that he had not lost *my* wife. Even though Elfrieda had been bedridden for a long time, I was depressed and lonely and knew that no one could totally relate to my experience. Depression and the feeling of isolation are common emotions after the death of a spouse, but no two people have exactly the same feelings.

I have observed a variety of grief reactions among various friends of mine who have lost a mate. I am reminded of Eloise, who witnessed the death of her husband at age sixty-six. She was sixty-three at the time. About a month after the funeral, she mentioned to me that she now was going to take some long trips with her friends on the Fun Tours bus. For the past forty-two years she had not been able to do so for three reasons: her husband disliked riding on a bus, he thought that trips were a waste of money, and he just didn't like to leave his easy chair and television. At a certain level she grieved over his departure, but she also felt now that she could do things she had never been able to do before. Strangely, there was a sense of freedom for her.

Harold, another friend of mine, displayed a very different type of grief. He and his wife had been to Europe three times and to South America twice, and had made at least a dozen long trips in the United States. When he found his wife dead of a massive stroke at age seventy-two, he was devastated. He became deeply depressed and needed professional help from a physician to help him overcome his deep grief.

As you can see, Harold and Eloise both experienced grief, but its effect on them was quite different. In summary, no one has ever experienced precisely the kind of grief you have. Don't try to conform to a rigid set of standards. Get good advice from a coping group, pastor, or professional counselor and shape your life so you can develop a maximum and meaningful life experience.

5. *God has not deserted you.* When someone is taken from us after sharing our lives for many years, there is a tendency to feel that God's loving power has deserted us. Keep this in mind: God still loves you. Romans 8:38–39 tells us: "For I am sure that neither death, nor life, nor angels, nor principalities, nor things present, nor things to come, nor powers, nor height, nor depth, nor anything else in all creation, will be able to separate us from the love of God in Christ Jesus our Lord." You should not let your depression cause you to doubt God's existence or to believe that God is paying attention to everyone but you. Even Jesus had that intense feeling of isolation when he was on the cross and cried, "My God, my God, why hast thou forsaken me?" (Matt. 27:46).

6. *Time and patience will be partial relievers for your present hurt.* Although it seems impossible to you at the moment, God has a way of using time to heal our wounds. We must believe and understand that our heavenly Father is all-wise and all-good and has a master plan for our lives. The death of a mate may seem to be both untimely and unfair, but be assured that God will be with you for the remainder of your life, however long it is. Our only hope in this and all other afflictions is to keep in mind the many promises God has given us and to trust that they will all be fulfilled.

7. *You should not expect any words of comfort that come from friends or relatives to reverse your grief suddenly and miraculously.* Losing a mate whom you deeply cared about is somewhat akin to having an accident in which you break several bones. You feel intense pain and shock throughout your entire body. In such situations, no thoughtful person can imagine an overnight cure for the difficulty. Although the pain does eventually subside and the hurt slowly heals, you have scars left to remind you of this traumatic event.

Will life ever be the same? Of course it will not be. You can never replace the mate you have lost, because no one else has his or her identical physical or emotional characteristics. Recently, Rita and I encountered a seventy-year-old widow whose husband died five years ago after a brief illness. She was still having a very difficult time dealing with her grief, because she had been very dependent on him. During the conversation, she mentioned that she might remarry "if only I could find a man like my first husband." The truth is, there *is* no man anywhere that is exactly like her first husband! To seek endlessly for such a person is an utterly hopeless undertaking and will hamper her chance for future happiness.

8. *The age of a mate when he or she dies has little to do with the amount or kind of grief you may encounter.* My

grandmother died at age eighty-four after a short illness, and I recall that several of our friends and neighbors remarked to my parents and me that we really should not feel bad, because she had lived a long and rewarding life. They advised us to simply accept her death, but there was the underlying message that any visible grief would give the wrong signal to a certain friend who had recently lost a loved one at a much younger age. Age has absolutely no relationship to how we should feel about the loss of a loved one. If you are well past middle age, do not let others minimize the painful significance of your mate's death. Your situation may be different from that of a younger person, but the hurt is just as intense.

9. *Your loved one did not die because it was "God's will."* Similarly, you are not being punished because of some sinful activity you have committed. Even though a close Christian friend may tell you that it was within God's plan to take your mate's life, it is impossible for any human to understand the will of God in the present life. Believing that a death was God's will may actually cause some survivors to become angry with God and thus make him the target of their wrath.

On one sad occasion, a young couple was en route to their regular Sunday service with their three school-age children. Their car struck a patch of ice on the highway and collided with a large bridge railing. The couple escaped with minor bruises, but all three children were thrown from the car and killed instantly. The four hundred people who attended the funeral service no doubt had a difficult time accepting the circumstances of the tragic event. In such a situation and at other times of grief, we should keep in mind comforting Bible verses. For example, Jesus tells us in Matthew 28:20, "I am with you always, to the close of the age." We have the constant assurance of his love and everlasting comfort, regardless of what happens in our lives.

10. *The grief resulting from the death of a mate may tempt you into believing that your faith was not strong enough.* A close friend alluded to our own belief system by suggesting that if we had possessed stronger faith, Elfrieda or Dick would still be with us. This type of statement is most unfortunate. Not only is the individual who says it presuming a knowledge of God's intentions, but he or she cannot be entirely sure about the depth of the listener's faith. Even in the New Testament, we note a reference to this subject when Martha says to Jesus that Lazarus would not have died if Jesus had been there (John 11:21). We should not place ourselves in the position of judging another person's faith or understanding God's plan. You are probably well aware of numerous situations when a loved one or acquaintance has been seriously ill and has not survived, even though dozens of deeply faithful persons had prayed for recovery.

11. *You should not expect your friends and relatives to undertake impossible tasks with regard to easing your grief.* Many people will say, "If you need anything, just let me know." There are many things that they cannot, in fact, do. They cannot replace the love and affection that your deceased mate brought you, nor can they fill the many lonely hours you encounter. If there are specific things that friends *can* do, however, you should tell them. Perhaps you need someone to take you shopping or to church services, to accompany you to a social function, or just to be your friend in many different situations. Caring people will feel useful if you let them do what they can for you.

12. *Some of your friends may try to lessen your grief by making statements to explain the death of your spouse.* I was told by a neighbor after my wife's funeral that she was now in a "better" place and that I needed to get on with my life. My friend was trying to comfort me. As a fragile human being, I was angry with God for taking her

from me. I wanted her with me. Implied in such a statement is the thought that I needed to shed grief as fast as
possible and act natural again. You are no doubt as lonely
as I was. You have lost a companion and are powerless
to do anything about it.

A lady in Mike's Sunday school class told him that
Susan had lived a long, full life and was "ready to go."
When someone we love is gone, it is difficult to dismiss
our memories of them and pretend they deserve less grief
than another person who has left us. Don't let anyone
minimize the importance of the life of your mate. No one
can take his or her place. For example, you may eventually remarry, but the new spouse cannot possibly have
the same characteristics as your departed spouse.

Ralph witnessed his wife's death at age fifty-nine from
a fast-moving brain cancer. They had been married for
thirty-eight years and were very close. From a casual
observer's vantage, they appeared to have a perfect marriage. He was mired in intense grief. A well-meaning friend
told him that the best way to overcome his grief was just
not to talk about it. He was of the impression that if you
didn't talk about your troubles, you wouldn't think about
them, and thus you would feel better. This is faulty logic.
Talking about the weather or last night's basketball game
will not erase Ralph's grief. My advice to you is this: If
you want to talk about your grief, do it. Your friends who
love you unconditionally will understand.

Sometimes in the case of a younger person, a friend
will say, "You are young and I am sure that God will lead
you to another husband." This statement has many negative connotations. It implies that every person must be
married and that total happiness is impossible without
a mate. There is a suggestion that there are many available men who are just like your late husband. Immediately after the death of a mate, remarriage is no doubt
the last thing on many people's minds. As noted in chap-

ter 6, we do not insist that remarriage is necessary or needed for every person.

Natalie related to me that she was told by her secretary, "You will get over it—it just takes time." People who say this to you somehow have the feeling that grief will last for a rather specific period of time and that once that time has elapsed, your grief will evaporate. The fundamental fact is that a large majority of surviving mates will grieve for a lifetime at some level. I still grieve for my dear mother who died over twenty-five years ago! Time has not erased her memory from my mind.

The wife of another professor died after a lingering illness at the age of sixty-two. I attended the viewing and lingered to converse with other friends in the gathering. I overheard a lady tell my friend, "Be thankful you had her for forty years." At least four people told me the same thing during the viewing for my late wife. While this is taken as a caring remark from a friend, it is pretty hard to be grateful for *anything* when you are in intense grief.

Many people say things to grieving people and think they are helpful. Consider carefully your reaction as illustrated by the situations just described. The best thing your friends can do for you is to tell you that they love you and are praying for you. Don't allow yourself to become confused or guilt-ridden from the trite phrases and utterances of those around you. In most cases they are well meaning, but they may not be very helpful to the griever.

In summary, grief is an emotion that every human being will encounter. To cry and feel depressed over the death of a mate is both natural and expected. You should not try to stifle expressions of your sorrow, because unresolved grief can lead to tragic physical and emotional disabilities. Healing will be facilitated if you follow the guidelines suggested in this chapter.

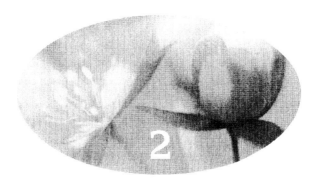

Caring for Your Physical and Emotional Needs

*T*he death of your mate will greatly affect your physical and emotional health. Grieving can cause numerous physical manifestations, such as headaches, dizziness, insomnia, moodiness, and various appetite problems. When reminders of your departed loved one cross your consciousness, anxiety and panic attacks may occur, manifested by irregular heartbeat, shortness of breath, trembling hands or feet, among other symptoms. Most physicians agree that there is a direct link between physical health and one's mental and emotional state. Mental health authorities have discovered that prolonged and unresolved grief can actually cause physical disabilities that may indirectly become life-threatening.

One of the most common complaints of grieving spouses is difficulty in establishing a regular pattern of restful sleep. A professor friend of mine recently witnessed the long and painful death of his fifty-three-year-old wife. He found that he awoke several times during the night with "flashbacks" of the many wonderful times that he and his wife had enjoyed. On other occasions those sleep disturbances bore reminders of the occasions when his afflicted wife needed him to move her to another location in the bed.

Other widowed persons we have interviewed complain that they are prone to awaken at a very early hour, such as three or four o'clock in the morning. One dear lady said she cried herself to sleep each night because she was now sleeping alone for the first time in thirty-seven years.

There are a number of ways of attempting to cope with these and related problems. First and most important, it is helpful to recall certain verses and promises that God Almighty has given us. Always recognize that there are countless conditions and situations, such as your mate's death, over which you have little, if any, control. Human explanations and remedies cannot remove your present grief. No amount of advice from your friends that "you need to get on with your life" will resolve your problems. Unfortunately, too many people (including faithful Christians) use the resources found in God's Word as a last step in helping them in their present need. To help you with your sleep and other physical problems, you can remember special promises that God has given us. For example, read Deuteronomy 31:6, Matthew 7:7, and John 14:14. Your pastor can suggest many other relevant Scripture passages.

In addition, to care for your present physical and emotional needs, you need to take a number of specific steps. Listed below are some practical things that you should do immediately.

Get a complete physical examination.

A thorough examination by a reputable physician can yield considerable information about such matters as your pulse, blood pressure, heart action, the condition of your eyes and ears, and other facets of your health that are important to help you cope effectively with your grief. For example, the emotional stress of grief may cause a significant rise in blood pressure. If your blood pressure readings have moved consistently above 140/90, the physician may recommend medication. Untreated high blood pressure can create serious health problems, including strokes and kidney damage. Especially at this point in your life, you do not need the added prospect of such dire circumstances. Do not be afraid to talk directly to your physician and tell him or her exactly how you feel, both physically and emotionally. A caring, considerate, and competent doctor needs this information to help you with your difficulties. If your doctor is not understanding, find one who is!

Some recent medical studies point to the high incidence of depression among many people, but especially among those who have experienced an intense hurt such as the death of a spouse. The feelings expressed below are symptomatic of depression:

- Most of the time I am sad and afraid.
- I don't want people around me—I just want to be left alone.
- It is very difficult for me to concentrate on any subject.
- Many times I don't feel like eating.
- Usually I wake up three or four times during the night.
- Sometimes I feel like I have been a disappointment to many of my friends and relatives.
- When I awake in the morning I feel downhearted and discouraged.
- I have lost interest in making important decisions— I would prefer that other people tell me what to do.

There is good news for persons experiencing depression. It can be treated successfully in most cases. Your physician can no doubt advise you of treatment plans such as medication and/or counseling.

Recently Larry King, the famous talk show host, devoted an entire hour-long show to the topic of depression. Many famous people appeared on the show and told how they had suffered depression for years and now had made a major recovery because of a caring, competent physician who knew what they needed. Several new depression medicines have been cleared by the FDA. If you think you have a depression problem as a result of the death of your spouse and related matters, seek out a physician at once! If you don't know who to call, check with your local city or county medical society about recommendations for a physician in your area. Help is waiting for you.

Think about whom to turn to for help if you become ill, now that your mate is gone.

The following people may be the most logical ones to contact: your children who live in the vicinity; brothers, sisters, or other relatives who are locally available; persons from your church or Sunday school class; friends or neighbors; a city or county visiting nurse association or private agency.

Visit with appropriate people on the list and prepare a plan before there is a need. In the next chapter, we talk about moving to a new location as "insurance" that persons will be available when you need them. (My parents lived on a farm some distance from the nearest hospital and doctors. When my father died in 1967, my mother bought a small home in a nearby town where help was readily available to her.) Consult your attorney about the advisability of executing a "durable power of attorney," which will allow a trusted family member or other person to pay your bills and make decisions on your behalf if you become ill or mentally impaired.

Finding a reliable, fair attorney requires much study and care. Visit with some of your friends and ask for the names of attorneys who deal with legal matters regarding estates and related items. If you have a legal association in your area, you can ask them for referrals.

Many reputable, established lawyers charge fees beyond the reach of some people. But sometimes an initial visit is free. At that appointment be sure to ask what his or her fees are for writing legal documents. If you cannot afford the fees, you may wish to contact your local legal aid society, which provides legal assistance for those persons with limited incomes. Your local county attorney's office may provide information about these services.

Make some plans regarding your own death.

You may place your name on your deceased spouse's gravestone, assuming that you will be buried beside him or her. If you make this plan, you should recognize one or more ramifications. What happens if you place your name on the headstone now, but later remarry? If you do remarry, you must decide whether to be buried beside your first or second mate. Also consider that you may move several hundred miles away for the remainder of your life. The family may then find it advisable to bury you at the place where you last lived, unless you have made definite plans about your final resting place as a part of your will or related instructions.

At the present time, a few people are choosing cremation instead of a traditional funeral. One of the obvious advantages of cremation is the cost. A cremation and a memorial service for the deceased may be realized for as little as $2,000, whereas an average traditional service is now in the range of $5,500 to $7,000. Costs vary depending on where you live. When considering cremation, there are many factors to analyze, such as your personal and religious beliefs as well as those of your close family members.

Many funeral directors supply information sheets to interested persons for recording their exact wishes. In my case, I have noted such details as where my service is to be conducted, what songs are to be sung, and what type of service I want. Although this may be too intense and troubling to many readers, I have recorded these data to save my family from major decisions upon my death. You may check with a local funeral director and consider it as a possibility.

Don't let your present age dictate what you should do. If you are relatively young, you may contend that you have many years to make such personal decisions. However, we have no guarantee of how many years we have left. If you do it now, you can update the information in your funeral director's office periodically. Make these decisions as soon as it is practical, and leave clear-cut instructions for whoever will be executor for your estate. Also review your own will and revise it if necessary.

Decide what to do with your mate's personal property.

We interviewed a number of widows and widowers about this matter and discovered that there was no one standard guideline or set of criteria that seemed applicable to all situations. After reviewing various aspects of this matter, however, we suggest that you keep in mind the following recommendations:

1. *Try to dispose of clothing and related personal items (cosmetics, shoes, purses, and wallets) in three months or less.* You may wish to invite your children, other relatives, and friends to select certain items that they may desire. If the idea of the clothing being worn by another person is too painful, you may wish to donate all items to your

favorite charitable organization or church mission. (The fair market value of articles donated to charities is tax deductible, so ask for a receipt.)

There are a number of reasons for this recommendation. First, the clothing is of no use to you and might be needed desperately by an acquaintance or an organization. Second, these items are a constant reminder of the mate and the fact that he or she will never return to wear them. Third, because fashions change, the clothes may not be practical for use by others at a later date.

Part of a healthy grieving process is making a sensible transition from living with a mate to learning how to cope alone without constant physical reminders of your loss. Rita and I know of a couple whose seventeen-year-old son was killed suddenly in a pole-vaulting accident during a track meet. The event happened almost four years ago, yet to this date, they have not touched an item in his room. This is a classic example of refusing to deal with grief and of "denial"—the total inability to accept the inescapable fact that their son will never return. These parents need to make the transition from the past to the present as quickly as possible. And so do you.

2. *There are other items (such as one-of-a-kind pictures, awards, plaques, letters, and jewelry) that you may want to keep indefinitely.* Looking at photographs of your deceased spouse may be a source of comfort to you. If you have children, you may wish to share some of these items with them now or designate who you would like to have them after your own death. You may keep expensive jewelry in a lockbox, but place selected pictures in various parts of the home if you wish. You may decide to put away pictures and other reminders of a deceased spouse if you remarry. A new mate may find it uncomfortable to see the pictures on an everyday basis.

Two brief case studies that illustrate the wisdom of disposing of one's personal items before death may suggest some strategies for you.

Each time we visit Mary, my ninety-four-year-old mother-in-law, in a distant state, she has a number of items ready for Rita to bring home. In most cases, it involves pictures of Rita when she was young and poses of Rita's children in earlier years. She has rightfully concluded that there should be a very small collection of items to be divided following her death.

Henry, a widower and a fellow bowler in my league, has gone to the trouble of writing the names of persons to receive items on the back of the articles for all to see. He has given duplicate copies of his wishes to all concerned relatives. He wants to avoid misunderstandings later.

The dividing of a person's belongings often becomes an acid test of the love and goodwill among family members. It has been my unfortunate experience to have witnessed several episodes of this type. Invariably, sister-in-law Betsy insists that, "Mother told me I could have that quilt and I want it." Daughter Evelyn believes that Mother never said such a thing, and an unfortunate scene takes place. This situation could have been avoided if the mother had divided most of her personal items before she died.

Get emotional support from a pastor or other counselor.

As mentioned in chapter 1, it is not a sign of weakness or mental illness to seek counseling on a temporary or regular basis. It has been our experience, however, that many pastors simply do not have time in their schedules to be involved in a sustained series of counseling sessions. The best avenue for you might be to seek out a community mental health center or pastoral counseling agency for either sustained individual therapy or participation in a support group where members share mutual concerns. Your personal physician may be able to refer you to a counselor or to a group that holds sessions for individuals who are experiencing grief. In any case, you need to acknowledge that there are many facets of your life that you cannot control, and that the resulting anxieties that you are presently experiencing may not go away unless you allow yourself to be helped by a professional counselor.

Accept help offered by family and friends.

But also be realistic about just how much support they can give you. The answer to this varies considerably from person to person, depending on the number of family members involved (and where they live) and on the type of your nonfamily relationships. The size of the town and the type of neighborhood in which you live have a direct correlation with the amount of help you may receive from people other than relatives. Typically in a small town and in close-knit neighborhoods, people know each other rather well and are prone to be attentive to the needs of their neighbors.

Rita and I are involved in a number of community service projects that involve people who have witnessed the death of a spouse. I am saddened and amazed at the number of people who have not developed a circle of friends—in fact some have not even spoken to close neighbors for two or three years! Because they have not reached out to people, they have no network of friends and hardly anyone knows them. Some live to themselves, attend church very infrequently, and prefer a hermitlike existence.

If the previous paragraph resembles your situation, do something about it right now! Regardless of your age, get involved in church and community groups. Volunteer if you can. Attend community programs, and let other people get acquainted with you. You will have much difficulty in this life if you live alone and have no network of support. To *have* a friend, you must *be* a friend.

You must realize that you cannot expect unlimited help from your family and friends. During the intense bereavement period just before the funeral and for a short time after, family and friends tend to be attentive to the mourner's needs. But Rita and I both discovered that even though many people said, "Let us know if we can help," they returned to their own personal day-to-day schedules soon after the funeral and somehow expected that we should be able to function effectively on our own. What many people fail to realize is that a bereaved mate is in most need during the first few weeks at home, when the absence of the loved one is keenly felt and the person is very lonely. This is especially true during evenings and weekend periods. For many persons, Sundays and holidays are especially painful. They certainly were for us.

Our advice to you is to respond to the open-ended offers of your friends and relatives for help by letting them know when you need their support. During an especially painful day, you might call someone and invite him or her to your house for a visit and a cup of coffee. Not only do people get busy and need to be reminded of their good intentions, but they may be reluctant to infringe on the desire for privacy you may inadvertently convey. There are indeed times when you wish to be alone with your thoughts, but it is unwise to isolate yourself from your loved ones and the community at large.

Even though your friends and relatives may not be with you at the times you would like, there are several promises from God's Word that can be of considerable comfort to you during this period. The following verses may be appropriate for reading at this time: Philippians

4:6–7; Revelation 21:4; and 2 Corinthians 1:3–4. Put your complete trust in God's love and provision, whether or not you receive as much help from your relatives or friends as you might wish.

Seek out the help of leaders in your church.

In most churches, a deacon or elder "overseeing" program provides long-term help and comfort to bereaved or otherwise needy members. If you are handicapped in some manner, you may need someone to help you with errands such as shopping or banking. During special holidays, a church family might invite you for a meal and fellowship if they knew you would otherwise be alone. Let your pastor know what your specific needs may be.

One of the most reputable interdenominational Christian care groups, found in most larger cities of the United States, is the Stephen Ministry. It consists of committed adult Christians who are dedicated to providing love and emotional care for those who are hurting. The persons involved in this program complete an extensive training course. Your pastor may have information about how to contact the local Stephen Ministry directors. You can also receive information about the nearest group by writing to Stephen Ministries, 1325 Boland Street, St. Louis, MO 63117.

Maintain an unbroken relationship with the persons and activities related to your church and its organizations.

During our interviews, we encountered two widows who were about seventy years of age. Their husbands had died about two years before, and they both remarked that they could not bring themselves to start attending church again. How sad! This situation is most unfortunate, because if ever they needed to hear God's message of love and comfort, it is now.

Assuming an isolated life and engaging in self-pity will not help you to adjust to a new life. You should go immediately to your minister or priest and share your feelings, but also get involved! Teach a Sunday school class; join the choir or a prayer group. Perhaps you can help in the nursery. Remember that you are not the only widow or widower in the church. Sharing in Christian fellowship provides a healing balm for many wounded spirits.

If you are not presently attending a church, visit several in the area. There are loving, caring people right in your neighborhood who are waiting to visit and comfort you, but they cannot do so if you do not make yourself known. Talk to the minister of the church if you cannot drive or do not have a car. He or she can no doubt suggest a person who can help with transportation. Many churches have buses to take people to services. And I have never met people who have refused to take a newcomer with them to church!

In summary, make a careful assessment of your physical and emotional needs and secure the necessary help to cope with the grieving process. There are many persons available and willing to be of service, but you must make contact with these individuals. By blending the help of caring people with the special promises of God, you can considerably increase your coping abilities.

Making New Living Arrangements

*A*fter a mate dies, a significant issue usually arises regarding where the survivor will live. We received numerous responses to this question as we visited with different survivors. It was apparent in some cases that they had made the right decision, although others regretted their plans. Since each situation is different, the living arrangements made by one person may not be right for someone else.

Regardless of your present age, when your spouse dies there are numerous adjustments you will have to make in your new living arrangements. The information we have included under the questions below is primarily designed for an older survivor; however, we are very aware of young widows and widowers—some in the thirty- to forty-year-old category. The last question contains specific information just for the younger person.

Obviously, we cannot cover every topic relating to this subject; however, we have highlighted those areas thought to be most important to the dozens of surviving mates we interviewed. Since each case is different, you should seek additional information from a trusted friend or counselor. A careful analysis of these topics should help you to make the right decision regarding your choice of where to live in the future.

Should you live with your children or other relatives?

The answer to this question depends on at least four conditions: (1) the age of your children and whether they are married; (2) how long you would expect to live with them; (3) whether you would be comfortable living in a nonprivate atmosphere; and (4) the present state of your physical and mental health. Many years ago, it was expected that children would care for the parent who was left as a survivor. Today, however, there are few married children who are willing or able to accept this responsibility. In many instances both the husband and the wife work outside the home, and there is no one available if the parent needs assistance. In addition, today's families are highly mobile, and it is common for young couples to move three or four times during the first few years of their marriage.

If you are physically and mentally healthy, it is probably best to avoid the temptation to live with your children or other relatives. They need their privacy and you need yours! In some cases, a son-in-law or daughter-in-law may resent the intrusion of the spouse's parent in their home on a permanent basis. For many persons, one of the important aspects of adjusting to their new life is to maintain as much of their former environment as possible. Having your own chair, bed, and other familiar items may be essential for your happiness and security. To give up all of these and live in another person's home may leave you with an ongoing feeling of loneliness and depression.

If you do decide to live with a child or other relative, it would be best to insist on a "trial" basis. It may be well to keep your own home and all your possessions for a few months until you can see whether the new surroundings are satisfactory. If they are not, you can move back to your house.

Should you sell your home?

Your home is one of the major financial investments that you and your deceased mate have made. There are many pros and cons with regard to selling your house, since there are not only monetary but also emotional factors to be considered. In the final analysis, only you can decide whether it is advantageous to sell. Generally speaking, it is best to wait at least a year before making such an irreversible decision.

The following may be reasons *for* selling the house. First, you may need the money to support yourself or to pay expenses involved with your mate's death. Second, you may wish to give up certain aspects of home ownership, such as lawn mowing and snow removal. If a deceased husband always did these jobs, for example, the wife may find this an important consideration. Third, if your mate was ill at home for a long period of time, you may wish to sell the home to leave behind those unpleasant memories.

Conversely, there are reasons why you may *not* want to sell the house. First, you may have spent a considerable amount of money remodeling the home to your desires. Many real estate appraisers confirm that the seller cannot usually regain the full cost of remodeling in the final sale price of a home. Second, you may have supportive neighbors whom you have known for a long time and may be reluctant to leave. At this point in your life, you may not wish to go to an unfamiliar environment where you will need to make new friends. You may also find that your beloved pets are not welcome in some apartments or condominiums. Third, you probably will have difficulty finding a comfortable replacement house or apartment at today's inflated prices unless you sell your house for a large sum of money.

The decision to sell your house may be agonizing and therefore calls for you to seek the best possible advice from family members and friends. Since your aim is to find living quarters that will result in your maximum happiness and well-being for the rest of your life, however, the choice must be yours and should not be made impulsively.

Should you move to a distant location?

It is difficult to answer this question without the knowledge of certain facts. Since one of the goals of many bereaved mates is that of keeping the immediate environment intact, there appear to be many disadvantages to moving to a distant location, even if the move puts you closer to family members.

Moving away requires you to get acquainted with new friends and services, including medical facilities, job opportunities, shopping outlets, churches, and community or cultural activities. If you decide to move to a new location, you probably need a friend or relative who can serve as a contact person for helping you become associated with church and other support groups that will help make the transition easier.

Should you ask a friend to move in with you?

For many people, living with a friend can help dispel loneliness and depression. A friend, of course, cannot replace a deceased mate—although he or she can provide one-on-one companionship and accompany you to programs, luncheons, and other public gatherings.

For this arrangement to be satisfactory, the friend must share your interests and general lifestyle and have a caring spirit. Living with a friend diminishes your degree of privacy and confidentiality, so the friend must be completely trustworthy, highly ethical, and sensitive to your feelings. Any plans should be temporary until you both deem the living arrangements totally satisfactory.

Should you change occupations or retire?

Most counselors and psychologists believe that the loss of a mate is one of the most traumatic events in life. Many of these specialists believe that at least one year should pass before any major decision is made, including changing occupations or retiring. Generally speaking, the one-year principle is good advice for most bereaved people. Your usual work pattern is good therapy in most instances. Unless there are compelling reasons to the contrary, it would be best for you to continue your usual occupational duties for at least a year following your mate's death.

Should you move to an apartment or buy a condominium?

As noted previously, you should maintain as much as possible the home setting that existed before your mate died. Some of the people we interviewed regretted that they had bought a condominium or moved to a rental unit because many of their new neighbors did not seem friendly—and now they are lonelier than ever. The disadvantages of unsociable neighbors and lack of companionship may, for you, outweigh the advantages of having no lawn to mow or snow to shovel. Our real estate agent noted that condominiums are considerably more difficult to resell than houses, so your decision may be binding on your future.

On the other hand, purchasing a condominium or renting an apartment may be wise and appealing if you want the freedom to travel or engage in other activities without the maintenance hassles of owning a home. You can merely lock the door and not have to worry about mowing the lawn or maintaining the house, because the usual maintenance chores are taken care of (for a fee). If you are over fifty-five, you might also wish to investigate the option of moving to a "senior citizen" complex, where—for an initial capital investment plus a monthly fee—you will have your own apartment but also have the security of an on-site medical facility and perhaps some of your meals.

In many areas, there are apartments and condominiums designed especially for single people of all age groups. Some professional groups, such as the Omaha Education Association, own condominiums. Many teachers whose mates have died choose to live in a housing development where there are others with similar interests. You might consider this kind of living arrangement.

As a final recommendation, it is wise to visit with several widows and widowers who have moved to apartments and condominiums in the area and ask them how they feel about the decision they have made. In addition, you may wish to talk with a trusted, veteran real estate agent regarding his or her opinion about buying a local condominium or town home. Then weigh all of the information and take whatever action seems appropriate in your situation.

Should you take measures to make your home or apartment more secure?

Yes! Call a locksmith to have deadbolt locks installed, and give a key to an adult child, trusted friend, or neighbor. If you live in a multi-dwelling complex, suggest to the management that they install a security system. If, on the other hand, you remain in a house, consider the possibility of installing a security system, especially if you will be gone for long periods of time. With a security system, a person who enters the home must punch a series of secret numbers on a special device. If the person fails to use the right numbers, an alarm sounds and notifies the security company and sometimes the local police. If you live in a small town or rural area where the sheriff or police officers are not quickly available, the security company can wire the system to notify a designated friend or relative by phone that someone has entered the house. Many of these systems also have medical emergency alerts. One example of such a company is ADT Security Systems, which operates nationally in both large cities and rural areas. Names of other companies can be obtained by consulting the Yellow Pages of the telephone book.

If you are a younger person, what are some special considerations to remember when making new living arrangements?

As noted earlier, try to remain in your present house or apartment for several months or a year if it is possible or practical. If you have children, this recommendation is extremely important. The death of their mother or father is in itself a tremendous adjustment. They do not need the added burden of moving to a new area and making new friends. This is especially true if you have lived in your present environment for several years.

Resist the temptation to move in with relatives or friends or have them move in with you. Eventually, you will have to make some firm decisions about future, long-term housing. Begin that journey now if you possibly can.

Many of the decisions regarding housing will center around your current budget. One of the most important things to do is to make a budget and determine to abide by it. You will obviously need to take into account the day-to-day necessities such as food, clothing, and housing.

Several options are available for housing. If your finances permit, there are apartments that are designed for young families. If you have children, this aspect may be very important because they can develop friendships this way. If you have very little money, you can investigate the possibility of low income housing in your area. Check with the social services department in your county. Contact real estate agents about rentals.

The location of your housing is extremely important. You may need child-care, thus you should live in close relationship to your child-care provider. You might also think of where close relatives live, so that in case of emergency they would be nearby to help you.

In addition to the above measures, you may ask a friend to call regularly to check on your well-being. You should keep a list of special phone numbers (fire, police, doctor) beside the telephone at all times. Now that you are living alone, it should be unnecessary to warn you to be extra cautious about admitting strangers to your home and leaving doors unlocked, whether or not you are there. Be sure to take the normal precautions about not "advertising" your extended absences, such as during vacation periods. Finally, your residence should have adequate smoke alarms—equipped with fresh batteries.

In summary, making appropriate plans for your residence is important to your overall happiness and security. You should try to maintain an atmosphere and setting as natural as possible and yet keep in mind that surroundings and relationships cannot possibly be the same as when your mate was alive. Most survivors should wait at least a year before making important decisions such as selling a home, buying a condominium, changing occupations, or retiring. Regardless of when you make any of these decisions, consult with trusted friends, counselors, and business persons, such as investment advisers and real estate agents.

Case Study # 1

George, age thirty-nine, was hauling some furniture in his truck for a friend. He noticed that a small cabinet had fallen off the vehicle and was tumbling to the opposite side of the road. He stopped the truck and ran to retrieve the cabinet. While doing this, he was killed instantly by a speeding motorist. He left Betty (age thirty-six and a tenured public school teacher) and three small children in Lincoln, Nebraska.

George and Betty were born in Kansas, and George's parents persuaded Betty to sell her home and move with her children "back home." The real estate agent sold her house in record time for cash, even though the selling price was less than the appraised value. At that point she moved all her belongings to a small house that she bought in her hometown of 1,500 people.

After making the move, Betty came to several tearful conclusions. First, nearly all of her old classmates of eighteen years ago had moved to Wichita and Hutchinson to find work. Three of her former girlfriends were still there, but they were married, had several children, and had no time for Betty. About the only friends she had were some older couples who attended her small Baptist church. Second, she could not find employment as a teacher because there were no immediate vacancies in area schools. The only job she could find was occasional babysitting. She was terribly frightened because she needed money to pay her monthly expenses and was too proud to ask for money from her in-laws. Third, as she thought of the possibility of marrying again, she soon discovered that the number of eligible bachelors was practically zero. Betty is still living in Kansas and is depressed and lonely.

Our Response: This is a classic example of a young, grief-stricken widow who bowed to the pressure of her well-meaning in-laws. It is obvious, as a matter of hindsight, that she should have stayed in Lincoln. She could have kept her teaching position and been with her friends. Before making any decision such as "moving back home," one should study every possible disadvantage as well as the presumed advantages. A mistake such as that made by Betty can be disastrous in more ways than one and is often difficult to reverse.

Case Study #2

Muriel's husband, Leland, died at age sixty-six shortly after he had retired as an oil company executive. They had lived in the same home for thirty-five years and were the parents of three grown children who were married and lived in the same city. Just ten years ago, Muriel and her husband had spent fifty thousand dollars to have their home completely remodeled and the yard land-scaped with new rose bushes and different shrubs.

Their oldest daughter, Ann, and her husband, Virgil, told Muriel that they had an extra room for her in their home and she could stay there for a modest fee each month. They contended it would serve two purposes: they would have a little more income, and Muriel would have someone around and would not be lonely. She gave in to their persuasion, sold her home, and moved in with her daughter and son-in-law.

Muriel soon found that it was a terrible mistake. When she drove by her former home and saw the beautiful shrubs and roses and visited with her old neighbors, she was heartsick. Her privacy in her daughter's home was practically nil. It was obvious that she had to conform to a schedule she did not like. She had a room to sleep in, but she did not have a *home*. Her daughter and husband had meals at odd hours, and their food was not to her liking.

Our Response: Muriel made a wrong decision. She should never have sold her home. It would have been much better to have kept her home while she lived with Ann and Virgil on a short-term, trial basis. If it did not work out, she could return to her home. Rita and I have known several people who have made a similar mistake. Moving in with relatives and friends can have many risks. Think carefully before selling your home.

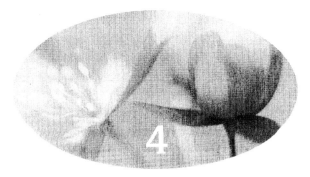

Moving Ahead with Your New Life

*I*n the previous chapters, we have advised you regarding your general physical and emotional needs and planning where to live. As time passes, there will be other aspects of living that need to be considered. I recently attended a workshop for persons who were planning to retire in the near future. Some members of the audience had made plans for their retirement years, whereas others had not. The speaker made the observation that days are just as long after retirement as they are during the working years.

One of the major challenges facing you as a survivor is how to make each day rich with contentment and personal fulfillment. Before your mate's death, you probably enjoyed many activities together. Unfortunately, you will discover (as I did) that today's society, with all of its activities, is basically designed for couples. A single person finds that he or she does not "fit" in many situations.

Now that you are single, it will be especially important to engage in meaningful activities that will provide a feeling of well-being and a sense of accomplishment. You have a set of experiences and (possibly) a work background that no one else has. Every person is gifted in some way. Just because your mate died is no reason for you to think that your uniqueness is no longer valuable to others.

This chapter will provide some ideas that have been useful for many survivors. Select one or more of these suggestions and use them as focal points for scheduling your daily activities.

1. *Search out those persons, agencies, and organizations that might need the services you can provide.* There are numerous admonitions in the Bible about providing service to others. You have special skills and talents that other persons need: "As each has received a gift, employ it for one another, as good stewards of God's varied grace" (1 Peter 4:10).

If you have the time, volunteering to work for various public agencies or private organizations can provide a number of satisfying advantages. Volunteer work can be an effective deterrent to the loneliness and depression that often accompany the grief caused by the death of a mate. You will meet new people who may have experienced (or will experience) the same kind of grief. You may also learn new skills that could be a forerunner to a new job or career. Finally, a regular commitment of time and effort will help you develop a renewed sense of self-worth and a structure in your routine. It is absolutely essential that you develop new purposes and strategies for understanding that life is worth living—even without a mate.

In developing a program of volunteer work, we have discovered that there are several important guidelines to keep in mind. First of all, decide in advance what kind of work you would like and how much time you can expend in volunteer activities. Be realistic and honest with the organization. Most agencies (such as hospitals and community organizations) expect a volunteer to work a certain number of hours each week or each month. Be careful about the assignment you accept, and do not make the mistake of agreeing to help out "whenever possible." There are specific demands inherent in any responsibility, and what one person may thoroughly enjoy might be highly stressful for another. For example, one hospital in our area accepts volunteers for at least four hours a week in the following areas: clerical assistant, intensive care lounge host/hostess or staff assistant, gift shop volunteer, bedside-shopping aide, dismissal escort, outpatient surgery or nutrition assistant, and rehabilitation therapy waiting area attendant. Some persons may find, for example, that working as a gift shop volunteer is more enjoyable and less taxing than working in the intensive care area.

Research fully the many different agencies that need the service of a volunteer:

Private and public schools (teacher's assistant, crossing guard, secretary's helper, lunchroom coordinator)

Culture groups (guides, telephone operators, and ticket sellers for museums, art and music centers, and the opera and ballet)

Hospitals and health and social service agencies (hospital worker, as noted earlier; Red Cross assistant; fund drive helper for the United Way, Salvation Army, and related groups)

Political and civic affairs groups (campaign worker for persons running for elective offices, assistant for League of Women Voters, leader for Boy Scouts or Girl Scouts or Big Brothers/Big Sisters)

Personal services (helping senior citizens with income tax forms and home repairs, sitting with persons with long-term health problems)

Churches (assisting with day care and Sunday school, custodial duties, and visitation). Your pastor can suggest many other activities.

2. *You are never too old to learn.* If your deceased mate provided most or all of your income, it may be necessary for you to undertake appropriate training or course work to enter the job market or to refresh your professional skills. The following are examples of friends of ours who restructured their lives after the deaths of their mates:

- John's wife died at sixty-five—just two years after they both had retired from teaching. He decided he wanted to work with lawyers, so he took the necessary courses and is now a paralegal assistant.
- Betty became a widow at age forty-three when her husband died in a car accident. She had never worked outside the home. Betty enrolled in a local university, and four years later she obtained her degree and certification as an elementary teacher.
- Joan's husband was accidentally electrocuted at age thirty-two. She was left alone with three small children and no skills. Joan found a neighborhood babysitter and attended a community college for two years, earning her certificate as a dental hygienist. She is now working for a prominent dentist.

After you decide to learn new skills, you must take into account a number of considerations. First, talk to counselors in a local university or college about career opportunities. They can suggest various tests you can take that will help you decide where your vocational aptitude and interests may lie. (For example, if working with groups of young children makes you anxious, you should not consider teaching or child-care occupations.)

Next, decide if it is possible to take the training locally or if you should attend a school some distance away that provides the necessary specialized courses. Of course, you must correlate the chosen program with the amount of money you have available for such activities. Be sure to investigate your eligibility for loans and scholarships.

Finally, determine the amount of time you can budget for training, considering both your age and future financial responsibilities. If you are near retirement age, it would probably be best to take a short training program to gain skills for earning money to supplement your Social Security income. On the other hand, if you are under forty-five, you may well consider a regular four-year college degree program. As a professor at the University of Nebraska at Omaha for twenty-five years, I had many students above forty years of age in my teacher-preparation classes.

3. *Consider taking some trips and excursions* (see also chapter 5). If your mate experienced a long, painful illness before his or her death, you probably did not recently have the opportunity to undertake any type of trips or vacations. (Elfrieda was very ill for the three years preceding her death, and we could not think of long trips.) A well-planned trip to enjoyable and relaxing surroundings may be valuable as a stress reliever. Since you probably need to take some time to meditate and relax among various groups of people, it may be advisable to avoid visiting an endless list of relatives. Although they mean to be kind, their conversations about events in the past that involved you and your deceased mate may be too stressful.

The key to planning and undertaking an enjoyable trip is finding a travel agent who is knowledgeable about the best fares and vacation sites. You might strongly consider going with a group on a domestic or foreign tour.

Group rates are usually less expensive, and the people going on the trip may be friends and neighbors, although that is not a prerequisite. Generally, taking several short trips is preferable to one long trip, at least until you discover whether you enjoy traveling.

In addition to commercial travel agents, you may secure valuable information from the nearest office of the American Automobile Association. For the annual fee, a member can receive detailed information about group tours or, if you prefer traveling on your own, road maps with the best trip routes. The association also sells insurance and provides a number of other services.

Other travel tips that might be helpful include the following:

- Make economical housing arrangements while traveling, staying at economy motels, "bed and breakfast" places, and guest houses.
- Use toll-free 800 numbers when arranging for hotel and motel reservations, and use your credit card to guarantee reservations.
- Bring along copies of prescriptions, extra pairs of glasses, and supplies of hard-to-find medicines. (Information concerning special medicines and/or vaccinations that may be needed for travel to a foreign country may be obtained from your physician or local health service.)
- Ask about the amount of walking required on the trips you have tentatively selected. (Climbing the Great Wall of China is not enjoyable if you have leg or joint problems!)
- Investigate Elderhostel classes that combine travel with short-term academic programs. Catalogs may be obtained by writing to Elderhostel, 80 Boylston Street, Suite 300, Boston, MA 02116, or by calling 617 426-7788.

4. *Start a new hobby or interesting pastime.* If your deceased spouse was ill for an extended period, it is possible that you had a limited amount of time to pursue leisure activities. Data secured from our interviews with survivors indicate that learning a new hobby, game, or sport has significantly helped to alleviate loneliness and grief.

The following is a list of hobbies that might interest you: pottery or ceramics, jewelry making, woodworking, sewing or knitting, drawing or painting, music, or theater. Even older persons can pursue a new sports activity such as bowling, fishing, tennis, golf, or volleyball if they are in good general health.

Many school districts and community colleges have noncredit courses and workshops that provide appropriate training and lessons in different hobbies and games. Tennis courts, bowling establishments, and golf courses usually have professionals available for giving lessons to those learning a new sport. Engagement in these activities will provide you with an opportunity to make friends and enjoy the excitement and challenges connected with new endeavors.

During the past seven years, I have been bowling in a senior's league. One week the four men on the opposing team were ninety-two, eighty-five, eighty-four, and eighty years of age. At seventy-one, I was the "kid" of both teams. These men have been bowling for years and enjoy it immensely. One man has been a widower for thirty years, but he has developed good exercise habits, maintained a large network of friends, and has enjoyed life in general. He could have stayed home, become depressed, and felt sorry for himself. He chose another path for his life.

Another interesting hobby for many people is using the Internet. Besides finding information to help in the healing process, you will find opportunities to converse with others. There are many prayer groups on the Internet, such as the Network of Prayer Warriors on America Online, whose members will pray for you while you are coping with your loss. The group members relate to each other and share a common bond of prayer for each person's needs. If you are anxious about using the Internet, ask a friend who regularly uses it to help you.

5. *Establish a regular program of exercise to make you feel better and improve your outlook on life.* Particularly at this stage of your life, you need to do everything possible to lower your anxiety and improve your overall physical and mental health.

Walking at a brisk rate for at least twenty minutes a day can dramatically improve your cardiovascular system and thus improve heart action, lower blood pressure, and stabilize heartbeat.

Swimming is also highly recommended by doctors, since many parts of the body are involved. Swimming increases muscle tone, joint flexibility, and coordination. This sport can be useful for all persons, from young children to senior citizens who are over eighty years.

If you are physically able, the addition of jogging, cycling, or low-impact aerobics to your list of leisure-time activities is prudent and healthful because they involve the major muscles of the body and can vitalize the cardiovascular system. If you do not wish to perform these exercises alone, you can join a group of persons in your age group. Information regarding such groups is available from your local Y.M.C.A. or Y.W.C.A. office or from a health club. A word of caution: *Always* consult your doctor before beginning an exercise program.

Regular exercise is an important ingredient for keeping your weight at a proper level. I recently attended a lecture by an exercise specialist who said that too many people who have suffered trauma such as the death of a loved one have difficulty with appetite, either eating too much or too little. If you have either lost or gained considerably in body weight since your spouse's death, a proper program of exercise and stress-reducing activities may be in order. If you live in a larger city, most private health and fitness clubs have personal trainers available for each person who is enrolled. A professional trainer designs an individual program of exercise just for you, considering your present age, weight, amount of body fat, and overall physical condition.

If you live in a small town or rural area and don't have access to health clubs, you can still engage in some type of meaningful exercise. Take a brisk walk down a country road for at least thirty minutes twice a day. The walk can be more enjoyable if you wear a headset radio and listen to your favorite program. If you are too far from a radio station for reception, buy a headset for use with tapes.

In addition to walking, you might investigate the purchase of a stationary exercise machine such as a treadmill. These items can be expensive, thus you should buy one with the option of returning it in thirty days if you don't like it. Remember to consult with your physician before undertaking these or any kind of major exercise program.

Dr. Kris Berg, an exercise professional at the University of Nebraska in Omaha believes that nearly every person is capable of engaging in some kind of exercise. He has programs for older people in wheelchairs and those in nursing homes. He contends that exercise should be a part of one's life until physical death occurs. Those who decide to be "couch potatoes" are more likely to contract health disorders of some kind.

According to Dr. Berg, physical activity provides countless benefits physically and psychologically. It adds years to your life, and life to your years. It strengthens your muscles, bones, heart, and lungs. It fights obesity, heart disease, type II diabetes, arthritis, and several types of cancer. Exercise builds self-confidence and self-esteem and fights depression.

Can anyone legitimately claim that he or she does not have the time to walk thirty minutes a day, even if it's done in several ten-minute mini-sessions? Can we afford *not* to exercise daily?

A half hour of moving the body daily is one of the best things we can do for our health. It can also be one of the most pleasant and relaxing things you do most of the days of your life. As the Nike commercial phrases it: "Just do it!"

6. *Try an activity that you have been afraid to do before, such as learning to drive a car or riding in a plane.* If you have never learned to drive, you could now take the opportunity to learn this skill. Overcoming your fear of driving can greatly reduce your dependence on others for providing transportation. You will not only learn a new skill, but you can also later help others who cannot drive. There are driver training schools in most cities. In a small town or rural area, your high school principal will have information about adult driver education classes.

Perhaps you have always had a fear of flying. Many people refuse to take long trips because of their anxiety about getting in a plane. Now that you are alone, you may wish to take a long-needed vacation to a distant place. Many airline companies offer classes and workshops for persons who fear flying. Call a local travel agency to find out if such classes are available in your area.

7. *Make a special effort to help others who are bereaved.* You are in a position to share your experience with others, including any special thoughts and verses from the Bible that have been very helpful to you. A Christian bookstore will have at least one book or cassette tape with an appropriate message for the bereaved person you are visiting. (Perhaps a copy of this book would be appropriate!)

In addition to the verses already pointed out in this volume, you may wish to emphasize promises such as the following to the person you are consoling:

> Psalm 46:1. "God is our refuge and strength, a very present help in trouble."
>
> Psalm 145:18. "The LORD is near to all who call upon him, to all who call upon him in truth."
>
> Isaiah 41:10. "Fear not, for I am with you, be not dismayed, for I am your God; I will strengthen you."
>
> James 4:8. "Draw near to God and he will draw near to you."

Service to other grieving individuals will help them and will provide a feeling of well-being for yourself. When ministering to others, be sure to share with them the promise that God loves and strengthens them in every situation, including both happy and sad times. Each of us is God's child, and God's perfect love is everlasting. He has promised never to leave us, forsake us, or leave us comfortless (John 14:18).

8. *Do not become a hermit by indefinitely confining yourself to your home following the death of your mate.* You need to get out of the house, visit with friends and relatives, go shopping, or at least take walks. The longer you sit at home, the more difficult it will be to get started with the activities needed to fill the void left by your spouse's death. Calling friends to accompany you can be especially therapeutic.

There are many roads to follow to make life interesting and fulfilling. If you are not already working, you may want to take a part-time job as a way to meet new people. Examples of "sociable" jobs are hostess in a restaurant, clerk in a small shop or store, or food-sample interviewer in a supermarket. For many people, immersion of one's self in such activities is an excellent reliever for grief and general anxiety. In other words, you need to get involved again in the world outside your door.

Your life can witness to others and may be the only "Bible" that someone will ever read. Let your faith be a light to people who are hurting. The way you handle your grief, disappointments, and hurts can be a positive influence, even on nonbelievers.

If you are to move ahead successfully with a new life, you need to engage in a varied program of activities to lower your stress level. At any stage of your life, you need to "take time to smell the roses." The following is a list of activities designed for relaxation. Select one or more and use them on a regular basis.

> Take the stairs instead of the elevator
> Laugh at yourself
> Visit a friend in the hospital
> Go to a playground and listen to the children yell
> Invite a friend to rub your back
> Receive a compliment without apology
> Listen to a symphony
> Take ten deep breaths
> Donate blood to the blood bank
> Go to a funny movie
> Sit in a hot tub
> Spend some money and buy some new clothes
> Look for something good in everyone you meet
> Get up early and listen to the quiet
> Each day, find three ways to help those less fortunate

In summary, let's review what we consider to be the major facets of building a new life after the death of your spouse.

1. *Get involved—find the names of persons and groups who need your services.* Check with the local AARP chapter or the county office on aging for suggestions. Your

pastor can no doubt tell you about several programs in the church that could use your help.

2. *Whatever your present age, you can learn new things.* Learning does not stop at fifty-five, sixty-nine, or even eighty-nine! I learned to bowl at age sixty-four. The beginning computer classes at our local community college are filled with senior citizens wanting to learn more about the Internet and World Wide Web.

3. *Try to lessen your stress level and engage in some relaxing, fun activities.* Get out of your house and take some trips, attend local free band concerts, and play bridge with some friends if you are physically able.

4. *Do everything you can to maintain a healthy body.* If you are not engaged in a regular exercise program, get involved today. A brisk walk can do wonders for reducing anxiety and tension. Join a health club if possible. Be sure you have your doctor's permission before starting a new program.

5. *Learn a new activity or skill.* For example, if you can't fix a simple appliance, enroll in a class at your local high school or community college. Keep your mind active to reduce the possibility of dwelling on your present grief on a constant basis.

6. *Try to reduce your stress level as much as possible.* Find several new and different activities that will enrich your life and make it more meaningful. *You can have victory, but it will take work and effort.*

Case Study #3

Marvin went to a local auction and upon his return home found his wife, age fifty-four, dead of an apparent heart attack. Efforts by the rescue squad professionals could not revive her. He and Sarah had just purchased a new motor home and had planned an extensive seven-state journey in the Rocky Mountain area. Her death was most untimely and created intense hurt among her three grown children and many relatives and friends.

One of their favorite activities had been singing at a local Saturday night activities center. Marvin was immediately struck with the awful fact that it was couples, not singles, who came to the events. What was he to do about getting on with a new life without Sarah, the new motor home, and their social schedule?

He took several actions to begin a new life. First, he asked his pastor if there were activities in his church that might be appropriate for a widowed man. The pastor recommended attending the men's prayer breakfast on Saturday mornings. To his amazement, he found that there were five other divorced or widowed men in the group who were close to his age. He began attending the sessions on a regular basis. He also went with a group of men on the church bus to the Promise Keepers convention in Minneapolis where he was involved with hundreds of men who had the same goals in life as he had.

Second, he decided to keep the motor home for the time being and use it for short trips to see a married daughter and her family in Colorado. He parked the motor home in their driveway and was thus able to keep his privacy and not interfere with the day-to-day living of his daughter, son-in-law, and three teenage grandchildren.

Third, he decided to alter his activities schedule in order to participate in "non-couple" activities. He was advised by the trainer in his health club to start including swimming in his exercise schedule. Each Tuesday and Thursday evening he went to the local Y.M.C.A. for swimming. There he found both men and women in his age range who were single as a result of death of a spouse or a divorce.

Our Response: Marvin took some positive actions to begin a new life. He soon found that there were other men right in his area who were in similar circumstances. He took some direct steps to restructure his life, such as listening to the advice of his pastor, friends, and exercise trainer. While life without Sarah will never be the same, he has designed a plan to realize a maximum amount of happiness and contentment for the remainder of his life.

Case Study #4

A police officer knocked on Pam's door at about four-thirty on a late summer afternoon to inform her that her thirty-four-year-old husband, Edward, had died of a sudden, massive heart attack while playing on the company softball team. They had been married for ten years, and he was a loving, devoted husband and father. Pam was devastated because she would not have help raising their three young children. She was in deep shock and could not understand why a loving God would permit such a thing to happen to her.

Pam's older brother Mack, a deacon in her church, was of tremendous help to her. Her grief was overwhelming, and she could not avoid a steady stream of tears at the viewing and funeral. It was obvious that she could not possibly restructure her life without the help of a caring counselor. Her pastor and her brother persuaded her to begin a series of counseling sessions at the grief counseling center at a local Christian university.

A retired banking officer in her church offered his help with advice about financial matters. Fortunately, Edward had a fifty thousand dollar life insurance policy. Her friend advised her about how to use the insurance money to help her in a maximum way with her house payments and other expenses. She followed his advice.

She was assistant teacher of her Sunday school class. The other couples of the class prayed with her and insisted that she keep attending the class even though she was alone. They invited her to the class Christmas party and the summer outdoor picnic. (*Readers:* The circle of friends and their support was the *key ingredient* in Pam's dealing with her husband's death. If you are without this kind of support, please get involved in a caring, believing church and see what a difference it makes. It is not too late!)

A year after Edward's death, Pam is still going to the twice-monthly conferences with her counselor. She has had many "down" days during the past year, such as Edward's birthday, their anniversary, Father's Day, and Christmas. However, her friends and the counselor have stood with her, and her level of pain and grief has lessened. Her hurt will be with her for life, but she is making progress.

Our Response: The timing of Edward's death was a great shock to his wife, children, and members of his church. Pam has been able to cope because she has a deep and abiding faith and has followed the wise counsel of her friends. She is making steady progress toward a fulfilling life.

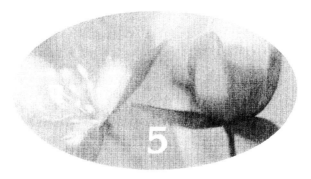

Handling Your Finances

*T*he death of a mate inevitably raises significant financial issues. You must, of course, perform a variety of related legal duties, including having your spouse's estate probated and changing the title on certain holdings, such as the family car, real estate, and financial instruments, if applicable in your case. Your monetary needs will be different, for example, if you are considering moving from the family home to an apartment or retirement complex; but this and other important decisions will be partially based on your knowledge of your financial situation.

You must find appropriate answers and data regarding the following questions, all of which will have an impact on your future security.

What are your present assets and liabilities?

In far too many cases, a mate has failed to leave a legally binding will and/or accurate financial records. We hope that is not the case in your situation. Even with a will, however, you may not be sure how much money is in the bank, in a savings account, or in stocks and bonds and other such holdings. As a general rule, you need a reputable attorney to help with probating the estate and listing your assets and liabilities. The county legal association and trusted friends should be able to suggest the names of lawyers in your area, if you do not have one already. You are also expected to pay all your mate's outstanding debts if you are to avoid legal action brought by creditors.

You (or some other person named as executor by either the will or the courts) are responsible for making the following information available to your lawyer or other adviser:

1. *Information needed to file appropriate forms relating to possible income (and estate/inheritance) taxes.* These data may include such items as IRS form 1099R and W-2 wage and tax documents. Your tax consultant will advise you of other needed information.

2. *A list of all investments and financial assets.* This includes insurance policies, money-market funds, certificates of deposit, stocks, bonds, amounts of money in employer annuity funds or retirement accounts, and appraisal of all personal and tangible property (for example, your home and other real estate, vehicles, boats). This listing should include notations as to which items were solely owned by your spouse and which were jointly owned by the two of you (with or without "right of survivorship").

Whether your mate's assets were solely owned or listed with you as co-owner, specific actions are required to accurately reflect the new ownership. Especially if there are other heirs besides yourself, it is important that all such documentation be handled legally and ethically. The executor of an estate is responsible for carrying out the provisions of an existing will—or for following the state's inheritance laws if a legal will was never drawn. You (or some other executor, if that be the case) should consult an attorney as to the necessary probate steps to be taken and to finalize any related transfer of assets.

For example, in the case of stocks and other tangible assets, whether or not you are co-owner, the issuing institution must be notified of your spouse's death so their records may be adjusted. This also applies to bank accounts and CDs. You will be advised of the necessary procedure and the documents required, which will probably include a copy of your spouse's death certificate and a court statement attesting to your (or someone else's) right to act as executor.

Ownership records may also need to be changed for "real" property, including real estate, cars, and possibly even your family home. In this regard, the experience of other surviving spouses points up the importance of having available as many official copies of the death certificate as may be needed at a future date. Most funeral homes will arrange to have these copies prepared for you as a matter of course for a nominal charge per copy. Inquire about this, since it is usually much easier to have these copies on hand than to secure them at a later date. Similarly, after the estate has been probated, you may wish to have copies of the applicable court certification drawn as soon as possible.

Obviously, there is a great deal of paperwork involved in all this! You may, of course, choose to handle some of these details on your own or with the help of family and friends. Even if you are named as executor, however, you can retain your attorney to attend to them on your behalf or to recommend someone who will. Although this may seem the simplest course, be aware that such administrative expenses usually mount up quickly and will, in the long run, deplete the size of your spouse's estate. If you do opt for handling some of the details, just be sure you know what you are doing. Consult your attorney before disposing of your spouse's assets to determine whether or not you hold clear title and can thus dispose of them as you wish.

3. *A composite listing of all debts and liabilities accrued by the deceased and the survivor to date.* This is especially important regarding installment loans, mortgages, and other liens that may be current and relevant to the estate, but also includes lump-sum accounts that may be due and payable in the future.

Is it necessary to retain the service of a certified public accountant and/or a financial adviser?

If the estate of your deceased mate is complex and involves numerous accounts and joint ownerships, the services of a CPA may be necessary. A specialist can best handle the payment of various taxes and is especially needed if many heirs are involved and if the will dictates distribution of certain funds. (The total charges paid to the CPA may be deductible as an expense on federal income tax returns.) Records and documents relevant to current income as well as a certified copy of present assets and liabilities can be presented to the lawyer and/or accountant to help in completing all the paperwork related to the estate and final income tax. (You may file a joint return for the year in which your spouse died.)

The employment of a financial adviser is, for most persons, a wise decision. If you have paper assets and income beyond Social Security and/or annuity checks, the correct placement of moneys is necessary to ensure that the best interest rates are obtained. (To complicate matters further, some interest income is fully taxable on both state and federal income tax forms; whereas other income, such as that from certain bonds, may be taxable at only one level. Some income is double tax-free.) Whether to place new or maturing investments in savings bonds, certificates of deposit, stocks, bonds, or gold depends on many factors and requires informed judgment by you and your financial adviser.

We should warn you that a few people who pose as "financial advisers" are, in fact, dishonest con artists who soon disappear after bilking their clients of large amounts of money. Some persons specialize in preying on the elderly or the bereaved, especially if the targeted "mark" appears to be uninformed about the world of finance. Before you retain the services of *any* adviser, try to determine if the person is well qualified and reputable. We recommend the following actions:

1. Ask for suggestions from close friends who have dealt with investment brokers and consultants.
2. Choose an adviser from a company that has been established in your area for a long period of time and is a member of a regional and/or national organization. (See #6.)
3. Contact the local Better Business Bureau for any comments, either positive or negative, about a given company.
4. After making an appointment to talk to a prospective investment adviser or broker, ask a trusted friend to accompany you. Later, compare your reactions about employing this person.
5. Study the number of companies represented by the adviser. The life savings that you and your mate have accumulated must be invested with great care. A competent specialist will explain the many options open to you, such as money-market certificates, stocks, municipal bonds, and certificates of deposit. You will need to have money immediately available even if you are able to afford long-term investments.

Since some of these options require a substantial penalty if any money is withdrawn before a given time, it is probably best to have money in both short-term and long-term investments.

6. Ask the person selected if he or she is a Certified Financial Planner. This national professional group requires its members to complete certain training each year to help ensure that their knowledge of financial matters is current and appropriate for their clients.

7. Analyze carefully the fees charged by the financial adviser. There are many types of fees charged by persons involved in financial planning. Some charge a flat yearly fee; others charge a commission for the purchase of certain stocks or bonds; others charge both an overall fee and a commission for their services. If the estate has a variety of assets and is large, seriously consider an adviser who charges a flat annual fee. On the other hand, if the estate is modest, a person who works on "commission only" may be more appropriate.

8. Once you have selected an adviser, be sure he or she understands your major objective, whether it be protection of principal, growth in value, or assured income. Above all, be wary of allowing the adviser to shift your investments without informing you, especially if the adviser's compensation is based on the number of transactions made.

As an additional caution, you need to be aware of "scams" being used against widows and widowers who appear to have a considerable amount of money. Recently, as program chairman for our local AARP, I asked our deputy county attorney to speak about "scams" and con artists operating in Omaha and other parts of the country. Below is a brief description of several of these dishonest actions taking place.

1. *"The pigeon drop."* Two women (or men) are visiting at the mall or on the street. A well-dressed man approaches them and tells them that he has found a large amount of money and points to what looks like many bills in a paper bag. He says he doesn't want to tell the police and would like to share the "money" with the two persons. They are asked to go to their banks and withdraw several thousand dollars in "good faith" money. When they return, they hand their money to the man and he gives them the "money" he found. The man leaves, and the people find the "money" was fake. They have lost a large amount of real money or even their life savings.

2. *"The bank examiner scam."* A pleasant, businesslike gentleman calls to say that he is a bank examiner and his agency has discovered that your bank officers have been dishonest. He is trying to prosecute them. He asks you to withdraw money and meet him at a certain location so he can take the money, redeposit it, and help catch the guilty bank officers. The man takes the money and is never heard of again. Hundreds of people have been bilked out of their life savings in this manner.

3. *"The car (or house) repair racket."* You are sitting on your front porch when a man in a van drives up and says he is a discount home repair person. He has noticed cracks in your driveway and house foundation blocks. As a "special" just for you, he offers all of the work for a mere $1,200, if you pay cash. You pay him the money; he puts some cheap caulking on the driveway and foundation and drives away.

A few dishonest car mechanics do the same thing. They say your car needs expensive repairs when there is little, if anything, wrong. Before you pay out any money, get a second opinion; and be sure the repair person is a well-established local person. If you are not sure of any of the details, check with a trusted friend or neighbor before having any work done to your house or car.

4. *"Consideration fee for prizes or vacations won."* Early one evening, Barbara received a call from a lady in a distant city who said she had won a round-the-world trip and was calling to congratulate her. She said that Barbara would need to send a $300 money order for the processing of her tickets for travel and lodging. Barbara sent the money order, and that was the last she heard from the "travel agent." Hundreds of these "boiler-room" operations are working actively to steal people's money. Remember: If you have won an honest prize from a reputable company, you never are charged a processing fee. Persons who engage in dishonest dealings of this type should be reported to any U.S. Postal Inspector if the solicitation is done by mail, or the Better Business Bureau if handled on the phone. (Also, you don't have to buy magazines to enter and win prizes by national magazine organizations.)

5. *"Special deals" by door-to-door salespeople.* A salesperson knocks on your door and says he has a new paint machine that will paint everything in your house. He has a one-day special just for you for a mere $800 cash. He insists on a demonstration. You are impressed and give him the money. You may have just purchased an ordinary $300 machine, and he has a quick profit of $500. Never give cash to any salesperson who comes to your door without an invitation. Insist on a sales agreement in writing. You have up to seventy-two hours to cancel a sale according to current law. Be sure you pay by check, and have the check stopped if your lawyer advises.

Be alert to these and other con artist schemes. Don't let your present grief lull you into making an unwise decision. If anything at all does not sound right, be sure to check with one or more trusted friends before writing checks or withdrawing money for anything. *Remember: If anything sounds too good to be true, it probably is.*

Do you need to buy additional insurance or make additional purchases at this time?

With the death of your mate, your need for future financial security is urgent, especially if you are no longer employed or have never worked. For example, you may consider a prepaid funeral plan that is offered by a local funeral home. If so, study all the details of such a plan and review it with a financial adviser or lawyer to determine if such a purchase is advisable.

You will no doubt want to purchase a suitable headstone for your spouse's grave if this has not already been done. Whether to obtain one stone with both names on it or to purchase two separate stones is a matter of individual choice. Local cemeteries and funeral directors can suggest the names of reputable companies.

It is vitally important to determine your present and future health insurance coverage. If your spouse had a group policy with his or her employer, that policy may no longer be in force for you without paying additional premiums. You may need to buy a new and different policy, depending on your age and thus eligibility for Medicare.

At the present time, many companies are selling policies to cover all or a certain amount of the expenses related to a stay in a semi-skilled or skilled care nursing home. Since some facilities may charge as much as $3,000 per month for their services, the purchase of such a policy may be both advisable and prudent. But before you buy such a policy, you should investigate the following questions:

1. What will the premium cost per month? (Comprehensive policies are expensive!)

2. What are the benefits of the policy? (Be sure to determine if custodial care for a disease such as Alzheimer's is covered.)
3. Is there a stated waiting period before the policy is in force? (Are preexisting conditions covered?)
4. Can the policy be canceled without notice?
5. What is the rating of the issuing company according to your state's insurance commissioner?

You should contact friends who have had direct experience with the insurance company and determine if the company and/or agent is long established and will be available immediately for consultation about questions that may arise later. Investigate carefully any company that sells policies only by mail or through advertisements in newspapers and magazines. Consult the insurance commissioner in your state capital about the reputation of such companies.

To minimize estate and inheritance taxes on your own estate, should you deed your property and other financial assets to a son or daughter (or some other person) and let him or her handle your future financial decisions?

While this plan may seem sensible and wise at the moment, it is full of pitfalls that may cause unbelievable problems later. Let us consider some of the possible developments:

First, suppose your child has a series of financial reverses and is forced to declare bankruptcy. In such a case, the property that was deeded to that child will no doubt be sold by the bankruptcy judge to satisfy the demands of creditors. Both you and your child would lose all benefits of the property.

Second, consider what happens if your son or daughter dies and the property is left to his or her mate, who may later remarry. The prospect of your retaining any rights to the property may be nil. (Consult a lawyer about how you might set up a trusteeship arrangement to prevent that situation.)

Third, the implications of conveying title to a child may have serious repercussions should it become necessary for you to enter a nursing home. Some people have the mistaken idea that they can deed almost all their property to another person and then immediately ask Medicaid to pay their nursing home costs. Be sure to consult a trusted lawyer for advice, since there is a considerable waiting period between the time of disposition of property and application for Medicaid benefits. (Eligibility rulings vary from state to state.)

We urge you not to let your present grief over the loss of a mate cause you to make quick and ill-advised decisions regarding your real estate or any other assets. Seek the help of a reputable attorney and/or financial planner who will have your best interests in mind.

Should you spend any of your current funds for trips or vacations?

For many people, a trip or vacation can be very helpful in lessening the intensity of grief and loneliness. A new surrounding can be soothing and comforting during the healing process, especially if it offers the opportunity to make new friends or renew old relationships.

Some persons cannot bring themselves to spend money in this manner because it seems somewhat frivolous or because they feel they may need the money later. During the past ten years, Rita and I have been grieved greatly by the untimely deaths of five of our friends before they reached retirement age. They ranged from ages forty-three to fifty-six and thus did not have the luxury of living to enjoy their golden years. The best advice we can give you is to take the trips and vacations that are financially possible now. It is later than you think! Of course, the decision regarding any substantial expenditure should be made with careful consideration of your financial situation and future needs. This is especially important for a grieving spouse, since your mixed emotions might impel you to act impulsively.

What should you do if you have only a small amount of available cash (or no money) when your mate dies?

There are several possible actions. You may borrow money against a house and/or insurance policy. Many banks also make modest, unsecured, short-term loans to persons with good credit records. Check with the local Social Security office about your eligibility for a burial-expense allowance for your deceased mate. (Also see the next question for other sources of funds.)

If you are totally without money, you should go to your county welfare office, the Salvation Army, the Red Cross, or your church for help. And don't be too proud to accept emergency loans from family or friends who offer to help.

It may be financially necessary for you to find employment as soon as possible, even if you have never worked outside the home before or your skills are "rusty." Local and state employment offices may list suitable job openings and/or training opportunities that will prepare you to enter the job market in the near future.

Be frank with yourself. You are the one who must take the above actions. There is help available, but you must find it. Even if a friend or relative accompanies you for emotional support, it is your responsibility to begin acting on your own behalf, even if you have rarely done so in the past.

Are there other sources of income, either lump sums or monthly benefits, for which you are eligible?

Explore all your possible options. The Social Security office is a good place to start. Besides the burial payment mentioned above, if you have minor children, it may be possible for them to receive support checks based on their deceased parent's earnings record. In addition, even if you are not yet old enough to be receiving benefits on your own, you may be eligible at age sixty to receive modest monthly checks—although these payments are dependent on the amount of your other income. It is worthwhile to check out this possibility.

The rules regarding Social Security, as well as SSI and Medicaid, are ever changing in response to new laws passed in Washington and in your state legislature. SSI is a program of additional income for persons earning below a certain minimum level. Medicaid is available for those with few assets who need funds for medical as well as other expenses. This program is available to all ages, not just senior citizens, and is administered directly by each state. For example, in many areas of the United States, more than half of all patients in nursing homes depend on Medicaid for their care. There are, however, well-defined rules for those receiving Medicaid payments. As noted earlier, you must thoroughly document the fact that you have very little money. You may not be able to deed your property to your children a month before entering a nursing home and qualify for Medicaid. Each case is different, thus you need to find information about the waiting period necessary between disposal of property and qualifying for Medicaid as it applies to *your* state.

For precise, current information about these programs, contact one or more of these offices: Social Security, county social services, state senator or representative, U.S. Representative, or U.S. Senator. Persons in these offices can either provide you with information or suggest where you can find the answers to your questions.

If you have Internet on-line service, you can contact various web sites in Washington for data regarding these topics. You may also contact your representative or senator by e-mail. Using these avenues, you may have a good chance of finding answers to specific questions in a short period of time. All congressional offices in Washington have large staffs. One of their major responsibilities is to answer questions from voters in their districts regarding Social Security, SSI, and Medicaid. Your tax money is paying their salaries—let them help you! Of course, you can also contact representatives and senators by phone, regular mail, and fax as well.

It is important to know all your rights as a surviving spouse. For example, if your spouse was a veteran, visit or phone the local Veterans Administration office and provide them with your spouse's service record, discharge papers, and data regarding any government insurance he or she may have carried. At the very least, the VA offers burial in a military cemetery or a one-time death benefit toward private burial. (Ask also about applying for an allowance toward a headstone if your spouse will not be interred in a military cemetery.)

Finally, if your spouse was already retired, you may be unaware of income for which you may be eligible. Check with the former employer's benefits office (and/or union, if applicable). Depending on your spouse's retirement package, you may be entitled to certain benefits—including a death benefit, insurance payment, monthly retiree checks, and/or medical coverage, as mentioned previously.

In summary, how you plan your finances will affect your present and future happiness and security. Following the advice offered in this chapter, along with recognizing that God cares for you now and forever, should help you considerably as you continue life's journey without your mate.

Case Study #5

David found himself a widower after his wife was killed in a tragic car accident. He was fifty-two at the time and was the father of three children, thirteen, fourteen, and seventeen years old. Lois had been an office manager for a large insurance company and had earned a salary of fifty thousand dollars a year. Their gross income had been over one hundred thousand dollars during the year previous to her death.

Her death meant some major adjustments for the family. They had to design a new plan of living to care for their individual needs. Lois had made the family budget and written nearly all of the checks. Fortunately, because of her excellent records, David found that he could determine what checks were to be written and when they were to be mailed. Besides the deep grief of her husband and children, they found themselves in financial trauma because it was the mother's salary that they had used to make the house payment and build college funds for the three children.

David took several commendable actions as a means of developing a new life:

1. He had a conference with his attorney and developed a plan of trusts for his children in case he died prematurely before they completed college.
2. Bart, the seventeen-year-old son, started working additional hours at the amusement park where he was employed. He earned

enough to take care of his personal expenses without having to ask his father for funds.

3. Kimberly, age thirteen, and Baldwin, age fourteen, decided that they would take responsibility for the major household tasks. They did their own laundry and cleaned the house thoroughly every two weeks.

4. David rearranged his schedule to be with his children for a maximum amount of quality time. The loss of their mother caused them to be lonely, and some crying spells came about. He dispensed with twice-a-week golf and instead spent the time with his children. The first summer after Lois's death, he accompanied all of the children to Disney World in Florida.

Our Response: David took some positive steps to structure his new life. He was mindful of the needs of his children and the financial demands of his family both presently and into the future. The grieving process of the children was helped tremendously by the desire on each family member's part to impart love to one another in a trying situation.

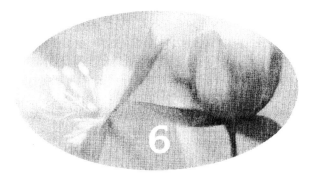

Contemplating Remarriage

*A*fter your spouse has been deceased for a period of time, you may think about the possibility of once again sharing your life with another. In practically every interview we conducted with widows and widowers of all ages, the question of remarriage was a common topic of conversation. (We have one friend whose wife died recently, who has had several unsolicited direct contacts from women who are "available.")

At the outset of this chapter, we wish to make it abundantly clear that even though Rita and I personally find remarriage to be satisfying, harmonious, and fulfilling, we do not wish to imply that all survivors should start an immediate search for a new mate. Many well-adjusted people may never desire to marry again. All knowledgeable people are well aware that marriage does not necessarily equal happiness, and it is better to be alone than to be involved in an unsatisfactory marriage.

This chapter is designed to give helpful information to those of you who are presently planning a remarriage or will become involved later with a person who may eventually become your new spouse. If you ever think of remarrying, read this material carefully. Even if remarriage is one of your major priorities and you feel it is God's will to follow this goal, there are numerous practical aspects to keep in mind.

Whatever you do, be sure that you are guided by the Scriptures in your pursuits. Surround yourself with prayer to help you follow God's will. We believe that God is Master of every facet of life and that, if you believe in his Word, every major step that you take—including remarriage—will be directed by him.

As part of the research for writing this chapter, we interviewed survivors who have remarried so that we could list criteria to consider before remarrying. Examine each item carefully. If you have difficulty resolving any of the questions posed, you need to examine more carefully your reasons for remarriage and your overall goals. The questions below are not listed in any order of importance, since each is vital to the success of your new marriage.

If you are interested in meeting new people with the possible view of remarriage, which avenues should you investigate?

Our interviews indicated that this was one of the most challenging questions faced by many survivors. (Persons from small towns and rural areas found few opportunities to come in contact with a wide range of persons.)

We first asked persons who had remarried, and then we asked various agencies for their suggestions. These are some groups and activities that you might explore for the purpose of meeting new friends:

They Help Each Other Spiritually (T.H.E.O.S.), large-city
   organizations whose members have experienced
   the death of a mate

church singles' groups (interdenominational) for both
   younger and older persons (check the church
   announcements page of your local newspaper)

senior citizens groups such as AARP, Golden Agers, and
   similar clubs for older people

bridge, bowling, golf, and bingo clubs and leagues that
   meet regularly

Elderhostel classes

national church camps (like those sponsored by the
   Southern Baptist Convention at Glorieta, New Mex-
   ico, and Ridgecrest, North Carolina) where various
   seminars and classes are held for those who are
   interested in a variety of church activities

adult education classes at local community colleges
   and universities

group tours in the United States and foreign countries

agencies (such as hospitals) that use the help of many
   volunteers

Christian pen pal organizations that advertise in many
   Christian journals such as *Christianity Today*

commercial groups, such as New Beginnings, that
   attempt to match your interests, needs, and values
   with another person of similar qualities through the
   use of videotapes and the computer

   Rita and I know of many happily married couples who met while involved in one or more of the previous groups. You must take action and make plans *now.* New friends or a possible prospective mate may be waiting to make your acquaintance. Trust in God to direct your path.

How long should you wait before you remarry?

The answer depends on a number of circumstances. Some authorities say that it should be at least a year after the death of your mate before you make *any* major decision, which certainly includes marriage. If the death of your mate was sudden, the resolution of your grief may be particularly difficult, and you may wait several years before even considering the idea of remarriage. Conversely, if your mate had a lingering illness and you went through a partial process of grief before his or her death, you may be comfortable in remarrying in less than a year. If this is true, the timing of your marriage may be of secondary importance. We are convinced, however, that resolving the answers to the next questions could take several months, or even years, for some individuals.

Do you have the same interests and values?

Having common interests (such as hobbies and leisure-time activities) and similar value systems (including political views and moral and spiritual values) is important. Much of the success of marriage is based on spending time together in conversation and on activities that are appreciated by both husband and wife. For example, if a husband likes to travel and the wife is a homebody, there could be possible stress on the marriage. Similarly, there should be considerable common ground on the major issues of life and the ability to communicate openly about them.

If there are children, how do they feel about your remarrying?

The issue was a serious one for Rita and me because she had four adult children and I had three. At first my children had only a slight acquaintance with Rita, and her children did not know me at all. After studying this question carefully and consulting counselors and trusted friends, we took a path that has been reasonably successful in establishing a harmonious family relationship. We recommend the following guidelines for your consideration.

1. *Introduce your prospective spouse to your children as early as possible.* Much of any initially negative reaction is because the individuals really do not know each other. If possible, let all the children in both families get acquainted before any marriage plans are announced. When you meet the children of your intended, be as natural as possible. Do not try to be someone you are not. They might not accept you completely, but if you show yourself to be a "phony," they will be even more suspicious. Especially if the children are young, respect them for who they are and be sensitive to their grief over the loss of the deceased parent, which may still be very painful to them. Avoid recommendations about child rearing to your intended at this stage. If his or her children make you uneasy or uncomfortable for any major reason, you had better have a serious conversation about your feelings. Even though it may be hard to accept, you will not only be married to this person, but you will also become involved with his or her children and other family members as well.

2. *Although the feelings of adult children regarding your remarrying must be considered, the final decision must be made by both of you according to the best interests of all.* Some children may be negative toward *any* relationship you enter because they may still be economically and emotionally dependent on you as a parent and feel isolated and neglected if you remarry or even consider doing so. A few people find it difficult to make adjustments in their lives and always prefer the status quo. On the other hand, if your children are opposed because of some specific loving concerns, consider these aspects

carefully. While you should be concerned about the feelings of your children, you need to take charge of your life and do what you believe is best for you. The most logical step is to discuss your children's reactions with your pastor or other counselor and some trusted friends who will keep the children's misgivings confidential. You need the opinions of persons who are somewhat detached from your situation and can give you objective advice about your relationship.

Once you are comfortable with the decision you have made, announce your intentions to your children privately and ask for their love, prayers, and goodwill. After you decide to remarry, most loving children will want your marriage to succeed and will be supportive. If not, the passage of time usually helps people to adjust to a new situation.

3. *Absorbing young children into a new marriage may be a major source of conflict for both of you.* When there are young children involved, assuming the stepfather's or stepmother's role may be demanding and traumatic. We have observed that a husband and wife may agree on nearly everything except how to raise children—their own or someone else's! It is nearly impossible to remain detached from such problems once a couple is united in a remarriage.

Often the family situation is still more challenging when you marry a divorced person and bring a child who has been living with the ex-spouse into your new home. Some children of divorced parents are very troubled and have a great capacity to spread discord wherever they go. Consider these possibilities seriously before remarrying.

Before you enter into a marriage where young children are involved, it would be advisable to air your concerns with your pastor and/or trusted friends. Don't let the present grief of your mate's death cause you to enter into a new marriage arrangement that is a profound risk for all involved.

Is your prospective mate understanding?

The matter of understanding and trust is extremely important in any relationship, of course. Think about the following questions:

1. Does he or she listen to you attentively and give you a chance to express your opinions and feelings?
2. Is he or she open-minded, rather than rigid and opinionated?
3. Is your intended willing to bend and compromise, rather than insisting on having his or her own way?

A negative response to even one of these questions can have serious consequences for a successful marriage. While you can never expect two persons to be in complete agreement about all issues, there should always be a climate in which you can reach a satisfactory compromise. A marriage is at risk when one person is dominant and the other is submissive only "to get along."

What is the financial status of each of you?

Of all the issues that may imperil a marriage, the subject of money can be the most deadly. The issues below must be studied and resolved *before* the marriage takes place.

Agreement must be reached if one of you has much more money than the other. There must be a clear understanding of how finances will be divided. There probably would not be a fifty-fifty split of assets in this circumstance. If this is a potential trouble spot, identify it early in a relationship.

A definitive plan must be established with regard to spending money—whether it be for yourselves, children's needs, recreation, vacations, or eating away from home. If you are planning to establish a joint checking account (with or without equal contributions to the account), there should be a clear understanding about which expenditures will be made from that source. Unless such a decision is reached, there is considerable potential for disagreement and stress.

A program must be agreed on with regard to checking, savings, and various investment accounts. The exact ownership and plans for these accounts should be described in detail in a prenuptial agreement (especially if either of you has children). Normally it is recommended that each of you keep your own name on any savings or investments that were yours before the remarriage. Decide whether the beneficiaries of the accounts will be your new mate or the children of one of you. Sometimes joint checking accounts are established with the understanding that both parties will contribute agreed-on amounts each month. For your mutual protection, property bought jointly after marriage should be stated on the title as "joint tenants with right of survivorship." (Also see next question.)

Should you have a prenuptial agreement and new wills?

The establishment of a prenuptial agreement before a second marriage is advisable, especially if there are children involved and if either of you has various financial holdings. In the event of a divorce or the death of one of you, each mate needs to have a clear understanding of his or her legal rights at that point. New wills are an absolute must so that each of you will know which possessions will be yours on the death of the other and to formalize your wishes regarding any other separate or joint heirs. Be sure that your will mentions that a prenuptial agreement has been made. If it does not, there can be considerable heartache for all concerned. Your county's legal society can recommend local lawyers who specialize in premarital agreements and wills.

What is the physical health of each of you?

You must be completely honest with each other regarding any present physical problems. We know of a couple who married about two years after their first mates died. Shortly after the marriage, the wife found that her new husband had concealed a long history of heart trouble. His subtle deception was a severe shock to her and was but one of the unfortunate reasons that they divorced a short time later.

Do you know the personal habits of the other person?

A loving, caring relationship requires a couple to live in a home environment where personal habits are agreeable and compatible. You should have definite knowledge concerning the following issues as they pertain to a prospective mate:

1. Smoking
2. Use of alcoholic beverages
3. Hobbies or leisure-time activities
4. Eating habits (food preferences, meal scheduling)
5. Sleep habits, both bedtime and rising
6. Personal hygiene
7. Friendship preferences, entertaining

While some of the above items may seem insignificant, one or more could be the source of stress in a marriage.

Of course, only you can judge whether your intended's habits will mesh with your own.

Are you sexually compatible?

One of the most important aspects of any marriage is the degree of sexual satisfaction attained by each member in the relationship. Your need for sexual gratification probably did not terminate at the death of your mate. Despite myths to the contrary, there is a substantial body of research data to show that the great majority of physically and mentally healthy persons remain sexually active up to age eighty and even beyond. If you intend to remarry, discuss your degree of sexual interest and your preferences in this area with your prospective mate. There is potential for a great amount of stress and difficulty if a person who has previously had a very active sex life marries someone who has little interest in sexual intimacy or has different ideas of how to express that intimacy.

What are your religious beliefs?

Of all the questions cited so far, this one may have the greatest potential for trouble between a couple. Resolve this issue before you pursue a relationship to any great depth. Our studies of this question have led us to some rather firm beliefs about three related concerns.

Basic spiritual values. If persons of any age (especially older) have never been interested in such matters as church attendance, tithing, prayer, witnessing, and the need to be saved, there is a good prospect that they will not embrace all or even some of these aspects just because they get married. We hope that they will change their lives. However, they probably will not.

Choosing a church. In the interests of harmony and general goodwill, it is desirable in most cases to agree on a church that you will both attend. There are all kinds of potential problems for younger couples especially, who attend different churches. These include how much money to pledge to each church, which church any children will attend, and how to deal with such fundamental theological issues as communion, tithing, speaking in tongues, and eternal life. Older couples can no doubt keep attending their respective churches if this arrangement is agreeable to both.

Evangelism in a marriage. The Bible tells us not to be "unequally yoked" with a nonbeliever (2 Cor. 6:14). To disobey this admonition may be an invitation to a stress-filled and unsuccessful marriage. Never enter a marriage with the expectation that your fervent witnessing will eventually lead your spouse to accept the gospel truths.

What will be your living arrangements?

There are many questions that need to be answered in this arena.

1. Will you live in the other's home or your own?
2. Will you both sell your houses (or move from your apartments) and buy or rent a new dwelling place that is jointly yours?
3. Will you have his or her children (and/or your own) living with you?
4. Will you use some of the furniture of each mate or buy everything new?
5. How will you dispose of items not needed in the new home?

Our experience and survey data show that there are no clear-cut, desirable answers for the previous questions. (Rita and I decided to live in her house, since she had lived there for twenty-three years and had recently spent a considerable amount of money remodeling it to her taste. We are using some of the furniture from my previous home. Pictures of our seven children are in a prominent place in the living room. Both of us are very comfortable with this arrangement.) Each situation has to be judged individually to arrive at a plan that will be satisfactory for both of you. If either of you is unhappy about living in the other person's house, you had best make other living arrangements.

Do either of you have family or financial obligations?

Discuss these details completely before the marriage takes place. Joe and Linda were married some time after the deaths of their mates. About one month after the marriage ceremony, during a casual dinner conversation between them, Linda discovered the following information about Joe's commitments:

He had told his mother she could live with them sometime during the next two years instead of going to a nursing home.

He was giving about $200 a month to his unmarried (and usually unemployed) son, who lived in the next town.

He had taken limited bankruptcy three years ago and still owed creditors over $20,000.

Obviously this information was most upsetting to Linda. These facts, along with Joe's refusal to compromise on certain religious issues, caused their later divorce. There should be no secrets of this type between two persons contemplating marriage!

Will you avoid comparison of your deceased mate with your new one?

You will never find a mate exactly like your first. Your new husband or wife will no doubt have some good (and bad) qualities that your first mate did not have, and vice versa. Do not place your former mate on a pedestal and challenge your new partner to be the same. Leaving the deceased's picture on the wall and constantly remarking that he or she "was so good" about doing such-and-such is not conducive to a harmonious second marriage. Conversely, there is no profit in amplifying all the faults of your former spouse. Be fair and objective about your first mate, without making direct or indirect comparisons to your new or intended partner. What happened in your first marriage is history—let it go at that.

If you have grown children, what will be your contact with them after you marry?

Your marriage will be a major adjustment for your adult children. If you follow some rather simple guidelines, your new marriage can be very successful.

First of all, let your children know that you still love them and that they should feel welcome to call you and see you within the bounds of common courtesy and good sense. Having a new husband or wife should not cause you to be isolated from your children, even if they have misgivings about the marriage.

Second, do not go to your children with every problem or conflict that you have with your new spouse, at least until all other avenues for resolution have been explored. Even then, it may be counterproductive to do so. In every disagreement have a private talk with your mate and try to resolve conflict at that level. Playing "mind games" with each other's children is a sure way of breeding major problems for a marriage.

How will you manage family traditions and holidays?

The first Thanksgiving and Christmas following a second marriage calls for much planning and discussion. There are many relatives to consider, and a calm, well-developed plan can avoid much unneeded stress. Keep as many of your own family traditions as you can, but at the same time be ready to compromise to include your new mate's relatives. You may need to have two Thanksgiving meals—or a big one for all. (Rita and I had all of our children and grandchildren for one big meal at Thanksgiving. It worked fine!) Can your traditions and celebrations be exactly the same as with your first mate? Of course not. But if both you and your new mate are flexible and willing to try new plans, family gatherings can be harmonious, fun-loving, and wholesome for all.

To summarize, we have emphasized that remarriage is not necessary or desirable for everyone whose mate has died. If you ask God's blessing and are led to the proper person, a new marriage can be highly rewarding. The questions in this chapter should be studied carefully before serious plans for remarriage are made.

Case Study #6

Bill and Helen had been married for fifty-four years when he died at the age of seventy-three. They had four grown children and all had been successful in their careers. Six months after his funeral, Helen remarked to me that she could not think of marrying again because no one could ever take the place of Bill. Her statement implied that Bill was fault-free.

Our Response: Though there is no man with Bill's exact characteristics, there may be a man with similar or even more favorable qualities. If Helen continues to maintain this attitude, she will forever foreclose any idea of a possible remarriage.

Case Study #7

Rusty and Arlis had been married for twenty-four years when she died unexpectedly of a brain tumor. Rusty was forty-six years old at the time and had two daughters, ages twenty and twenty-two. The oldest daughter, Melrose, stated in no uncertain terms that her father had better not even think of remarriage because to marry another woman would show great disrespect for her late mother. Rusty bowed to the wishes of his daughter, not wanting to incur her wrath.

Our Response: It is our view that Melrose is in error in thinking that remarriage is disrespectful. It is a compliment for two survivors who want to form a meaningful marriage. We believe that Rusty should not put his full trust in his daughter's opinion. It is Rusty, not Melrose, who is living a lonely existence in his house. If he is led to a suitable companion for the rest of his life, he should be encouraged, not criticized.

Case Study #8

Two years ago, Betty witnessed the death of her husband, Arnold, at the age of fifty-four. He had a lingering cancer for the last four years of his life and was bedridden for the last year before his death. During a recent conversation with Betty, she told me that she would never think of marrying again because she didn't want to live through an illness and death of another husband.

Our Response: The fact is that there are no human guarantees in this life. This matter, as well as other possible future events, are under the control of Almighty God who created us. Worry is the penalty you pay for disbelief. I tried to persuade Betty that she should take the chance to share her remaining years with a new mate if the opportunity presents itself. She should complete the Cushenbery Readiness for Marriage Inventory (see Appendix) and decide if the results are hopeful for her.

Case Study #9

Three years ago, Chuck's forty-year-old wife, Rachel, died in a commuter plane crash on the east coast. He was forty-two at the time, and her death was a great shock to him. They had no children. Since their marriage twenty years ago, they had been very active in a local fundamental church—she as the children's director and he as a deacon. During one of Chuck's Monday night outreach visits, he became acquainted with Sandra, a recent widow. Her husband had taken his life about two years ago. Soon they started visiting on the phone, and several months later the relationship arrived at a serious stage and they were married.

Unfortunately, their marriage lasted only ten months. What went wrong? She promised to start attending his church and stop her occasional drinking after they married. Since she was overweight, she intended to see a physician and start on a diet. None of these things happened.

Our Response: Our advice to all persons thinking about marriage is quite basic: *What you see is what you get.* People do change—many times for the better—but don't count on it. They should have taken our Cushenbery Inventory (see Appendix). The results would have alerted them both to potential trouble spots.

In light of the material presented in this chapter, we have prepared a short inventory to estimate the *possible* success of your proposed marriage plans. We call it the Cushenbery Readiness for Marriage Inventory (see Appendix). We wish to stress that this is an informal measure and is not designed to be used in place of other evaluations provided by a trained marriage counselor. The major purpose of the inventory is to alert you to some possible risks involved in marrying again. We do not wish to give the impression that every item is absolutely equal in importance. Our only contention is that any one of the items is significant enough to contribute to a failed marriage. If you have scores in the borderline, moderate risk, or high risk categories, you should definitely discuss these issues with a pastor or trained marriage counselor. Conversely, scores in the excellent and good ranges obviously do not guarantee a successful marriage, but they do give some positive indication that a lasting marriage is possible.

An Overview

*W*e have written this new revised book because we know that there are countless persons of all ages who have lost a spouse. The information has been compiled to help you cope with one of the most traumatic events to take place during your lifetime—the death of your husband or wife. Yes, he or she died, and now you are bereaved and hurting. We understand and sympathize. We hope we have helped you.

You have discovered with each passing day that the physical death of your mate was final. He or she cannot be replaced, even if you marry again. You may still be in a state of shock. When your mate died, you probably were not ready to accept that inescapable fact or anticipate all of its repercussions. At the moment my wife died, I was angry with God for taking her from me. I finally realized that God accepts such anger and knows it is a sign of the human frailty that we all have.

Like you, we have shed many tears, but we have come to realize that God loves us and knows our every need better than we do. He hears our innermost thoughts and our cries for help and—though our path seems narrow and crooked—he will provide a way. God's promises are true. When you feel lonely and depressed, remind yourself again and again that he is with you always, even to the end of the world. People may forsake you, but God will not.

Remember these important concepts:

1. *Grief is an emotion encountered by every human being.* To cry and feel depressed over the death of your mate is both natural and expected. Do not try to repress your grief, because unresolved sorrow can lead to tragic physical and emotional disabilities. If you trust that God loves you, he will give you the strength to carry on. His wisdom is infinite, and he knows the load you are carrying.

2. *The strategies you have undertaken for your present and future financial situation have a significant influence on your overall material security.* Now that your mate is gone, there are certain important steps that you must take, as noted in chapter 5.

3. *Carefully assess your physical and emotional needs and secure the necessary help that you may need to cope with the process of grieving.* There are persons such as your pastor and community mental health specialists who are available to help you. By blending their comments with the promises that God has provided in his Word, you should be assisted greatly in stabilizing and building your overall well-being.

4. *You are now confronted with making new living plans.* Your future happiness and welfare are at stake as you contemplate selling your home or moving to a new location. The important recommendations found in chapter 3 should be of help to you as you make these important decisions.

5. *Moving ahead with your new life means scheduling your time carefully to include hobbies, service projects, and*

personal-improvement activities that will be both mean-ingful and uplifting. You may now have time to study the Word more deeply and to reach out and witness to fellow human beings who are also hurting. Your faith and belief in God's teachings can be a source of comfort and renewal for those to whom you minister.

6. *You may be led by God's will to remarry at some later time.* Before pursuing any serious relationship with the goal of marriage, you need to study carefully the items that are discussed in chapter 6. Take the Cushenbery Inventory and see if there are any risks for remarriage. Rita and I have found our marriage to be satisfying and harmonious, but it is not our intention to convey the idea that all survivors should pursue this goal.

We hope this volume will inspire and help you as you pursue a new life after the death of your mate. Rita and I do not pose as trained clerics, psychiatrists, or psychologists. Our major qualifications are that (a) we have had the experience of witnessing the deaths of our mates, (b) we believe there are certain commonsense approaches that bereaved mates can use to carve out a new life, and (c) we are convinced that our goal in this life should be to study God's Word and follow it—especially as it relates to his will for the remainder of our time on this earth.

Life is a series of adjustments and bumps in the road. The death of your spouse was one of them. May God give you courage to carry on. We pray that his love will surround you this day and all of the days to follow.

Appendix

The Cushenbery Readiness for Marriage Inventory

*T*his informal subjective inventory is designed to acquaint a person of any age who is contemplating marriage with the possible strengths and risks involved with this decision.

Photocopy pages 104 and 105 so individuals can score the inventory in private. Intended spouses should check the items. The couple should then have a meeting and discuss their scores. If there is a difference, the couple should try to discover the reasons for it.

There are fifteen statements. Check each one as *true, undecided,* or *false.*

Scoring: Each *true* item counts three points; *undecided,* one point; and *false,* zero points.

Use the scale on page 105 for predicting the estimated success of your future marriage.

	True	Undecided	False
1. The person I am marrying is less than seven years older or younger than I.			
2. We have very similar religious views.			
3. We are both in good physical and mental health.			
4. Neither of us has been divorced.			
5. Both of us are believers and uphold the basic teachings of Christ.			
6. We have the same, or nearly the same, interests and lifestyle.			
7. Neither of us has large outstanding debts and/ or future financial obliga- tions (less than $1,000 excluding automobile and/or home mortgage).			
8. To the best of my knowl- edge, we have similar sexual interests.			
9. Our present and projected total income will be more than enough to pay our bills.			

	True	Undecided	False
10. Both of us have success-ful strategies for handling conflicts and problems.			
11. We have agreed on a tentative financial budget and savings plan for at least the next year.			
12. From what I have obser-ved, I expect to have a positive relationship with my future in-laws.			
13. We have discussed family traditions and how we will participate after we are married.			
14. Both of us have agreed on the kind of church we will attend.			
15. We have decided on the number of children (if any) we desire. (If beyond child-bearing years, mark True.)			
MY TOTAL SCORE:_____			

Prediction of Marriage Success:

Excellent (42–45)   _____
Good (37–41)   _____
Borderline (33–36)   _____
Moderate Risk (30–32)   _____
High Risk (0–29)   _____

If you are in the moderate or high risk categories, you should seek advice from a reputable counselor before proceeding with marriage plans.

Reading List

The following books may be helpful as additional reading. These volumes can be found in most larger Christian bookstores.

Connelly, Douglas. *After Life.* Downers Grove, Ill.: Inter-Varsity Press, 1995.

Deffner, Donald L. *At Life's End.* St. Louis: Concordia Publishing House, 1995.

Exley, Richard. *When You Lose Someone You Love.* Tulsa: Honor Books, 1995.

Froehlich, Mary Ann. *An Early Journey Home.* Grand Rapids: Baker, 1992.

Jensen, Margaret. *Who Will Wind the Clock?* Nashville: Thomas Nelson, 1993.

Robinson, Haddon W. *Grief.* Grand Rapids: Discovery House, 1996.

Sissom, Ruth. *Moving beyond Grief.* Grand Rapids: Discovery House, 1994.

Webb, Sylvia. *Saying Goodbye to Susan.* West St. Paul: J & S Publishing, 1993.

Wernecke, Herbert H. *When Loved Ones Are Called Home.* Grand Rapids: Baker, 1995.